The Life of Jesus

A Simple Narrative

WARREN RAVENSCROFT

The Life of Jesus: A Simple Narrative
© Warren Ravenscroft 2020

Cover Art: 'Compassionate Christ'
© Artist Kendra Parrish Burton 2012

ISBN: 979-8-88525-719-0 (paperback)

Bible passages from New King James Version Bible (NKJV)

Published by Warren Ravenscroft
Website: www.wittonbooks.com

A catalogue record for this
work is available from the
National Library of Australia

Contents

Foreword

The New Testament gospels tell us the story of Jesus' life and ministry. They give us the same story but from four different sets of eyes.

Gospel writers may have used different sources of information. They may have had different audiences for whom they wrote their story. But they wrote their story for one common purpose and that was to pass the message of Jesus to others, especially those who never saw Jesus in person, including our generation.

In 'The Life of Jesus. A Simple Narrative', Warren Ravenscroft sets out the gospel accounts of Jesus life in chronological order. This line of narration makes it easy for the reader to follow the story line. That the gospel is the story of a historical figure who ministered to the people of his era in the first century in Palestine.

The significance of the gospels is the message it portrays and the teaching it gives. However, the chronological order of this book will allow the reader to appreciate Jesus life-story as one single narrative and not four. This is especially so for those who like the art of orderly story telling.

The orderly format gives a fresh look and an insightful view of the story of Jesus, His life and ministry. I am reminded of the words of song writer, Arabella Catherine Hankey, (Salvation Army Song Book. 1986 edition. Song 98):

⁽¹⁾ *Tell me the old, old story*
Tell me the story simply
⁽²⁾ *Tell me the story slowly*
Tell me the story often
⁽³⁾ *Tell me the story softly*
Tell me the story always
⁽⁴⁾ *Tell me the same old story*
Christ Jesus makes thee whole.

It is my prayer and I'm sure the prayer of the author, that the book will help us tell the old story simply. That we will also tell the story slowly and often. That we will tell the story softly and tell it always. By so doing, Christ Jesus will make us whole!

God bless you each richly in your story telling.

Commissioner Andrew Kali

Territorial Commander.
The Salvation Army Papua New Guinea

Introduction

Over many years, I have studied similar gospel accounts of the same event, and then arranged or blended them into one passage containing all the facts. I found this enhanced the word to bring a rich and full meaning to what was taught or shared.

How often have we heard a sermon or completed a Bible study using one Gospel account only of an event, and later found so many other facts which had been missed because only one gospel was used.

Often, some significant saying or remark is overlooked when the word is shared with others. Many times, a very relevant part is glossed over. It is not until the complete account is finished, that the hidden message emerges, adds to but does not subtract.

It is for this reason, under the prompting and guidance of the Holy Spirit, I set my mind to first chronologically ordering all the passages and then blending together similar passages to obtain one complete narrative.

Having used the Chronological New King James Version as a guide, made it easier to find all the relevant passages.

An easy way to describe what was to be achieved is, under the guidance of the Holy Spirit, like making a four-ingredient cake. Matthew is the flour, Mark is the sugar, Luke is the egg and John is the sultanas. You place them all into a bowl, mix them together, and place them in a cake tin, allowing the heat of the

Holy Spirit to transform them into a cake, on the prepared table God sets before us.

I was pleasantly surprised to find that during the process of blending the Gospels, the Holy Spirit opened my spiritual eyes and understanding to many parts, although previously read, made an immense impact on the complete story, event or parable.

I would sit and reread what had been given to me, over and over to try and absorb the written word. What I was now reading, enhanced the meaning, taking me to a deeper spiritual level. The Holy Spirit had moved me from knowledge to understanding.

Some passages readily come to mind such as the calling of Andrew, Peter, James and John. The account of the Crucifixion. The Passover and the Last Supper. The women who attended to Jesus after the Resurrection.

A number of years ago, a friend presented me with a Bible. On the front page was written,

"Study to show yourself approved unto God,
a workman that needs not to be ashamed,
rightly dividing the word of truth". 2 Timothy 2:15

I believe that the Holy Spirit has enabled me to do exactly what Paul the Apostle advised Timothy.

All Glory to God.
Warren Ravenscroft

Spirit Filled
Life Study Bible
New King James Version (NKJV)

John 1:1-18

The Eternal Word

In the beginning was the Word, and the Word was with God, and the Word was God. He was in the beginning with God. All things were made through Him, and without Him nothing was made that was made. In Him was life, and the life was the light of men. And the light shines in the darkness, and the darkness did not comprehend it.

John's Witness: The True Light

There was a man sent from God, whose name was John. This man came as a witness, to bear witness of the Light, so that all through him might believe. He was not the true Light, but came only as a witness to the Light, that gives light to every man coming into the world.

He was in the world, and the world was made through Him, and the world did not know Him. He came to His own, and His own did not receive Him. But as many as received Him, to them He gave the right to become children of God, to those who believe in His name: who were born, not of blood, nor of the will of the flesh, nor of the will of man, but of God.

The Word Becomes Flesh

And the Word became flesh and dwelt among us, and we beheld His glory, the glory as of the only begotten of the Father, full of grace and truth.

John bore witness of Him and cried out, saying, "This was He of whom I said, 'He who comes after me is preferred before me, for He was before me.'"

And of His fullness we have all received, and grace for grace. For the law was given through Moses, but grace and truth came through Jesus Christ. No one has seen God at any time. The only begotten Son, who is in the bosom of the Father, He has declared Him.

Luke 1:1-4

Dedication to Theophilus

Inasmuch as many have taken in hand to set in order a narrative of those things which have been fulfilled among us, just as those who from the beginning were eyewitnesses and ministers of the word delivered them to us, it seemed good to me also, having had perfect understanding of all things from the very first, to write to you an orderly account, most excellent Theophilus, that you may know the certainty of those things in which you were instructed.

Luke 1:5-80

John's Birth Announced to Zacharias

There was in the days of Herod, the king of Judea, a certain priest named Zacharias, of the division of Abijah. His wife was of the daughters of Aaron, and her name was Elizabeth. And they were both righteous before God, walking in all the commandments and ordinances of the Lord blameless. But they had no child, because Elizabeth was barren, and they were both well advanced in years.

While Zacharias was serving as priest before God in the order of his division, according to the custom of the priesthood, his lot fell to burn incense when he went into the temple of the Lord. And the whole multitude of the people was praying outside at the hour of incense.

Then an angel of the Lord appeared to him, standing on the right side of the altar of incense. And when Zacharias saw him, he was troubled, and fear fell upon him.

But the angel said to him, "Do not be afraid, Zacharias, for your prayer is heard; and your wife Elizabeth will bear you a son, and you shall call his name John. And you will have joy and gladness, and many will rejoice at his birth. For he will be great in the sight of the Lord, and shall drink neither wine nor strong drink. He will also be filled with the Holy Spirit, even from his mother's womb. And he will turn many of the children of Israel to the Lord their God. He will also go before Him in the spirit and power of Elijah, *'to turn the hearts of the fathers to the children,'* and the disobedient to the wisdom of the just, to make ready a people prepared for the Lord."

And Zacharias said to the angel, "How shall I know this? For I am an old man, and my wife is well advanced in years."

And the angel answered and said to him, "I am Gabriel, who stands in the presence of God, and was sent to speak to you and bring you these glad tidings. But behold, you will be mute and not able to speak until the day these things take place, because you did not believe my words which will be fulfilled in their own time."

And the people waited for Zacharias, and marvelled that he lingered so long in the temple. But when he came out, he could not speak to them; and they perceived that he had seen a vision in the temple, for he beckoned to them and remained speechless.

As soon as the days of Zacharias service was completed, he departed to his own house. Now after those days his wife Elizabeth conceived; and she hid herself five months, saying, "The Lord has done this for me, in the days when He looked on me, to take away my reproach among people."

Christ's Birth Announced to Mary

Now in the sixth month the angel Gabriel was sent by God to a city of Galilee named Nazareth, to a virgin betrothed to a man whose name was Joseph, of the house of David. The virgin's name was Mary. And having come in, the angel said to her, "Rejoice, highly favoured one, the Lord is with you; blessed are you among women!"

When Mary saw him, she was troubled at his saying, and considered what manner of greeting this was. Then Gabriel said to her, "Do not be afraid, Mary, for you have found favour with God. And behold, you will conceive in your womb and bring forth a Son, and shall call His name Jesus. He will be great, and will be called the Son of the Highest; and the Lord God will give Him the throne of His father David. And He will reign over the house of Jacob forever, and of His kingdom there will be no end."

Then Mary said to the angel, "How can this be, since I do not know a man?"

And the angel answered and said to her, "The Holy Spirit will come upon you, and the power of the Highest will overshadow you; therefore, also, that Holy One who is to be born will be called the Son of God. Now indeed, Elizabeth your relative has also conceived a son in her old age; and this is now the sixth month for her who was called barren. For with God nothing will be impossible."

Then Mary said, "Behold the maidservant of the Lord! Let it be to me according to your word." And the angel departed from her.

Mary Visits Elizabeth

Now Mary arose in those days and went into the hill country with haste, to a city of Judah, and entered the house of Zacharias and greeted Elizabeth. And it happened, when Elizabeth heard the greeting of Mary, that the babe leapt in her womb; and Elizabeth was filled with the Holy Spirit.

Then she spoke out with a loud voice and said, "Blessed are you among women, and blessed is the fruit of your womb! But why is this granted to me, that the mother of my Lord should come to me? For indeed, as soon as the voice of your greeting sounded in my ears, the babe leaped in my womb for joy. Blessed is she who believed, for there will be a fulfilment of those things which were told her from the Lord."

The Song of Mary

And Mary said:

"My soul magnifies the Lord,
And my spirit has rejoiced in God my Saviour.
For He has regarded the lowly state of His maidservant;
For behold, henceforth all generations will call me blessed.
For He who is mighty has done great things for me,
And holy is His name.
And His mercy is on those who fear Him
From generation to generation.
He has shown strength with His arm;
He has scattered the proud in the imagination of their hearts.
He has put down the mighty from their thrones,
And exalted the lowly.
He has filled the hungry with good things,
And the rich He has sent away empty.
He has helped His servant Israel,
In remembrance of His mercy,
As He spoke to our fathers,
To Abraham and to his seed forever."

And Mary remained with her about three months, and returned to her house.

Birth of John the Baptist

Now Elizabeth's full time came for her to be delivered, and she brought forth a son. When her neighbours and relatives heard how the Lord had shown great mercy to her, they rejoiced with her.

Circumcision of John the Baptist

On the eighth day, those who were chosen, came to circumcise the child; and they would have called him by the same name as his father, Zacharias.

His mother answered and said, "No; he shall be called John."

They said to her, "There is no one among your relatives who is called by this name."

They made signs to his father, asking what he would have him called. And he asked for a writing tablet, and wrote, saying, "His name is John."

They all were amazed. Immediately his mouth was opened and his tongue loosed, and he spoke, praising God.

Then fear came on all who lived around them; and all these sayings were discussed throughout all the hill country of Judea. And all those who heard them kept them in their hearts, saying, "What kind of child will this be?"

And the hand of the Lord was with him.

Zacharias' Prophecy

Now his father Zacharias was filled with the Holy Spirit, and prophesied, saying:

"Blessed is the Lord God of Israel,
For He has visited and redeemed His people,
And has raised up a horn of salvation for us
In the house of His servant David,
As He spoke by the mouth of His holy prophets,
Who have been since the world began,
That we should be saved from our enemies

And from the hand of all who hate us,
To perform the mercy promised to our fathers
And to remember His holy covenant,
The promise which He swore to our father Abraham:
To grant us that we,
Being delivered from the hand of our enemies,
Might serve Him without fear,
In holiness and righteousness before Him all the days of our life.
And you, child, will be called the prophet of the Highest;
For you will go before the face of the Lord to prepare His ways,
To give knowledge of salvation to His people
By the remission of their sins,
Through the tender mercy of our God,
With which the Dayspring from on high has visited us;
To give light to those who sit in darkness and the shadow of death,
To guide our feet into the way of peace."

And the child grew and became strong in spirit, and was in the deserts till the day of his manifestation to Israel.

Matthew 1:1-17

The Genealogy of Jesus Christ

The book of the genealogy of Jesus Christ, the Son of David, the Son of Abraham: Abraham begot Isaac, Isaac begot Jacob, and Jacob begot Judah and his brothers. Judah begot Perez and Zerah by Tamar, Perez begot Hezron, and Hezron begot Ram. Ram begot Amminadab, Amminadab begot Nahshon, and Nahshon begot Salmon. Salmon begot Boaz by Rahab, Boaz begot Obed by Ruth, Obed begot Jesse, and Jesse begot David the king. David the king begot Solomon by her who had been the wife of Uriah. Solomon begot Rehoboam, Rehoboam begot Abijah, and Abijah begot Asa. Asa begot Jehoshaphat, Jehoshaphat begot Joram, and Joram begot Uzziah. Uzziah begot Jotham, Jotham begot Ahaz, and Ahaz begot Hezekiah. Hezekiah begot Manasseh, Manasseh begot Amon, and Amon begot Josiah. Josiah begot Jeconiah and his brothers about the time they were carried away to Babylon. And after they were brought to Babylon, Jeconiah begot Shealtiel, and Shealtiel begot Zerubbabel. Zerubbabel begot Abiud, Abiud begot Eliakim, and Eliakim begot Azor. Azor begot Zadok, Zadok begot Achim, and Achim begot Eliud. Eliud begot Eleazar, Eleazar begot Matthan, and Matthan begot Jacob. And Jacob begot Joseph the husband of Mary, of whom was born Jesus who is called Christ.

All the generations from Abraham to David are fourteen generations, from David until the captivity in Babylon are fourteen generations, and from the captivity in Babylon until the Christ are fourteen generations.

Matthew 1:18-25, Luke 2:1-7

Christ Born of Mary

Now the birth of Jesus Christ was as follows: After His mother Mary was betrothed to Joseph, before they came together, she was found with child of the Holy Spirit. Then Joseph her husband, being a just man, and not wanting to make her a public example, thought he would put her away secretly.

But while he thought about these things, behold, an angel of the Lord appeared to him in a dream, saying, "Joseph, son of David, do not be afraid to take Mary as your wife, for that which is conceived in her is of the Holy Spirit. And she will bring forth a

Son, and you shall call His name Jesus, for He will save His people from their sins."

All this was done that it might be fulfilled which was spoken by the Lord through the prophet, saying: *"Behold, the virgin shall be with child, and bear a Son, and they shall call His name Immanuel,"* which is translated, "God with us."

Then Joseph, being aroused from sleep, did as the angel of the Lord commanded him and took Mary as his wife, and did not know her till she had brought forth her firstborn Son.

And it came to pass in those days that a decree went out from Caesar Augustus that all the world should be registered. This census first took place while Quirinius was governing Syria. So, all went to be registered, everyone to his own city.

Joseph also went up from Galilee, out of the city of Nazareth, into Judea, to the city of David, which is called Bethlehem, because he was of the house and lineage of David, to be registered with Mary, his wife, who was with child. While they were there, the days were completed for her to be delivered. And she brought forth her firstborn Son, and wrapped Him in swaddling cloths, and laid Him in a manger, because there was no room for them in the inn.

Luke 2:8-20

Glory in the Highest

Now there were in the same country shepherds living out in the fields, keeping watch over their flock by night. And behold, an angel of the Lord stood before them, and the glory of the Lord shone around them, and they were greatly afraid.

Then the angel said to them, "Do not be afraid, for behold, I bring you good tidings of great joy which will be to all people. For there is born to you this day in the city of David a Saviour, who is Christ the Lord. And this will be the sign to you: You will find a Babe wrapped in swaddling cloths, lying in a manger."

And suddenly there was with the angel a multitude of the heavenly host praising God and saying:

"Glory to God in the highest, and on earth peace, goodwill toward men!"

When the angels had gone away from them into heaven, the shepherds said to one another, "Let us now go to Bethlehem and see this thing that has come to pass, which the Lord has made known to us."

And they came with haste and found Mary and Joseph, and the Babe lying in a manger. Now when the shepherds had seen Him, they made widely known the saying which was told them concerning this Child. And all those who heard it were amazed at those things which were told them by the shepherds. But Mary kept all these things and pondered them in her heart. Then the shepherds returned, glorifying and praising God for all the things that they had heard and seen, as it was told them.

Luke 2:21-38

Circumcision of Jesus

And when eight days were completed for the circumcision of the Child, His name was called Jesus, the name given by the angel before He was conceived in the womb.

Jesus Presented in the Temple

Now when the days of her purification according to the law of Moses were completed, they brought Him to Jerusalem to present

Him to the Lord (as it is written in the law of the Lord, *"Every male who opens the womb shall be called holy to the LORD"*), and to offer a sacrifice according to what is said in the law of the Lord, *"A pair of turtledoves or two young pigeons."*

Simeon Sees God's Salvation

And behold, there was a man in Jerusalem whose name was Simeon, and this man was just and devout, waiting for the Consolation of Israel, and the Holy Spirit was upon him. And it had been revealed to him by the Holy Spirit that he would not see death before he had seen the Lord's Christ.

On a certain day, Simeon came by the Spirit into the temple. And when the parents brought in the Child Jesus, to do for Him according to the custom of the law, he took Him up in his arms and blessed God and said:

"Lord, now You are letting Your servant depart in peace, according to Your word;
For my eyes have seen Your salvation
Which You have prepared before the face of all peoples,
A light to bring revelation to the Gentiles,
And the glory of Your people Israel."

And Joseph and His mother marvelled at those things which were spoken of Him.

Then Simeon blessed them, and said to Mary His mother, "Behold, this Child is destined for the fall and rising of many in Israel, and for a sign which will be spoken against (yes, a sword will pierce through your own soul also), that the thoughts of many hearts may be revealed."

Anna Bears Witness to the Redeemer

Now there was one, Anna, a prophetess, the daughter of Phanuel, of the tribe of Asher. She was of a great age, and had lived with a husband seven years from her virginity; and this woman was a widow of about eighty-four years, who did not depart from the temple, but served God with fastings and prayers night and day. And coming in that instant she gave thanks to the Lord, and spoke of Him to all those who looked for redemption in Jerusalem.

Luke 2:39-40

The Family returns to Nazareth

When they had performed all things according to the law of the Lord, they returned to Galilee, to their own city, Nazareth. And the Child grew and became strong in spirit, filled with wisdom; and the grace of God was upon Him.

Matthew 2:1-18

Wise Men from the East

Now after Jesus was born in Bethlehem of Judea in the days of Herod the king, behold, wise men from the East came to Jerusalem, saying, "Where is He who has been born King of the Jews? For we have seen His star in the East and have come to worship Him."

When Herod the king heard this, he was troubled, and all Jerusalem with him. And when he had gathered all the chief priests and scribes of the people together, he inquired of them where the Christ was to be born.

They said to him, "In Bethlehem of Judea, for thus it is written by the prophet:

'But you, Bethlehem, in the land of Judah,
Are not the least among the rulers of Judah;
For out of you shall come a Ruler
Who will shepherd My people Israel.'"

Then Herod, when he had secretly called the wise men, determined from them what time the star appeared. And he sent them to Bethlehem and said, "Go and search carefully for the young Child, and when you have found Him, bring back word to me, that I may come and worship Him also."

When they heard the king, they departed.

Now the star which they had seen in the East went before them, till it came and stood over where the young Child was. When they saw the star, they rejoiced with exceedingly great joy. And when they came into the house, they saw the young Child with Mary His mother, and fell down and worshiped Him. They opened their treasures, and presented gifts to Him of gold, frankincense, and myrrh.

Then, being divinely warned in a dream that they should not return to Herod, they departed for their own country another way.

The Flight into Egypt

Now when the wise men had departed, behold, an angel of the Lord appeared to Joseph in a dream, saying, "Arise, take the young Child and His mother, flee to Egypt, and stay there until I bring you word; for Herod will seek the young Child to destroy Him."

When Joseph woke from his sleep, he took the young Child and His mother by night and departed for Egypt, and was there until the death of Herod, that it might be fulfilled which was spoken by the Lord through the prophet, saying, *"Out of Egypt I called My Son."*

Massacre of the Innocents

Then Herod, when he saw he had been deceived by the wise men, was exceedingly angry; and he gave orders and put to death all the male children who were in Bethlehem and in all its districts, from two years old and under, according to the time which he had determined from the wise men. This fulfilled the prophesy which was spoken by Jeremiah the prophet, saying:

"A voice was heard in Ramah,
Lamentation, weeping, and great mourning,
Rachel weeping for her children,
Refusing to be comforted,
Because they are no more."

Matthew 2:19-23

The Home in Nazareth

Now when Herod was dead, an angel of the Lord appeared in a dream to Joseph in Egypt, saying, "Arise, take the young Child and His mother, and go to the land of Israel, for those who sought the young Child's life are dead."

Then Joseph left their home in Egypt, and took the young Child and His mother, and came into the land of Israel.

When Joseph heard that Archelaus was reigning over Judea instead of his father Herod, he was afraid to go there. And being warned by God in a dream, he turned aside into the region of

Galilee. And he came and dwelt in Nazareth, that it might be fulfilled which was spoken by the prophets, "He shall be called a Nazarene."

Luke 2:41-52

The Boy Jesus Amazes the Scholars

Jesus, with His parents went to Jerusalem every year at the Feast of the Passover.

And when He was twelve years old, they went up to Jerusalem according to the custom of the feast. When they had finished the days, as they returned, the Boy Jesus lingered behind in Jerusalem. And Joseph and His mother did not know it; but supposing Him to have been in the company, they went a day's journey, and sought Him among their relatives and acquaintances. When they did not find Him, they returned to Jerusalem, seeking Him.

Now after three days, Joseph and Mary found Him in the temple, sitting in the midst of the teachers, both listening to them and asking them questions. And all who heard Him were astonished at His understanding and answers.

When they saw Him, they were amazed; and His mother said to Him, "Son, why have You done this to us? Look, your father and I have sought You anxiously."

And He said to them, "Why did you seek Me? Did you not know that I must be about My Father's business?"

But they did not understand the statement which He spoke to them.

Jesus Advances in Wisdom and Favour

Then Jesus went down with them and came to Nazareth, and was subject to them, but His mother kept all these things in her heart.

And Jesus increased in wisdom and stature, and in favour with God and men.

Matthew 3:1-12, Mark 1:1-8, Luke 3:1-18, John 1:19-28

John the Baptist Prepares the Way

The beginning of the gospel of Jesus Christ, the Son of God. As it is written in the Prophets:

"Behold, I send My messenger before Your face,
Who will prepare Your way before You.
The voice of one crying in the wilderness:
'Prepare the way of the Lord;
Make His paths straight.'"

Now in the fifteenth year of the reign of Tiberius Caesar, Pontius Pilate being governor of Judea, Herod being tetrarch of Galilee, his brother Philip tetrarch of Iturea and the region of Trachonitis, and Lysanias tetrarch of Abilene, while Annas and Caiaphas were high priests, the word of God came to John the son of Zacharias in the wilderness. And he went into all the region around the Jordan, preaching a baptism of repentance for the remission of sins, as it is written in the book of the words of Isaiah the prophet, saying:

"The voice of one crying in the wilderness:
'Prepare the way of the Lord;
Make His paths straight.
Every valley shall be filled
And every mountain and hill brought low;

*The crooked places shall be made straight
And the rough ways smooth;
And all flesh shall see the salvation of God.'"*

Now John himself was clothed in camel's hair, with a leather belt around his waist; and his food was locusts and wild honey. Then the people in Jerusalem, Judea, and all the region around the Jordan, went out to John and were baptized by him in the Jordan River, confessing their sins.

A Voice in the Wilderness

Now this is the testimony of John, when the Jews sent priests and Levites from Jerusalem to ask him, "Who are you?" he did not deny, but confessed, "I am not the Christ."

And they asked him, "What then? Are you Elijah?"

He said, "I am not."

"Are you the Prophet?"

And he answered, "No."

Then they said to him, "Who are you, that we may give an answer to those who sent us? What do you say about yourself?"

He said:

*"I am the voice of one crying in the wilderness:
Make straight the way of the Lord,*

as the prophet Isaiah said."

Now those who were sent were from the Pharisees. And they asked him, saying, "Why then do you baptize if you are not the Christ, nor Elijah, nor the Prophet?"

John answered them, saying, "I baptize with water, but there stands One among you whom you do not know. It is He who, coming after me, is mightier than I, is preferred before me, whose sandal strap I am not worthy to loose. I indeed baptized you with water, but He will baptize you with the Holy Spirit."

These things were done in Bethabara beyond the Jordan, where John was baptizing.

John Preaches to the People

But when John saw many of the Pharisees and Sadducees coming to his baptism, he said to the multitudes that came out to be baptized by him, "Brood of vipers! Who warned you to flee from the wrath to come? For this reason, show fruits worthy of repentance, and do not begin to say to yourselves, 'We have Abraham as our father.' For I say to you that God is able to raise up children to Abraham from these stones. And even now the axe is laid to the root of the trees. Therefore, every tree which does not bear good fruit is cut down and thrown into the fire."

The people asked him, saying, "What shall we do then?"

He answered and said to them, "He who has two tunics, let him give to him who has none; and he who has food, let him do likewise."

Then tax collectors also came to be baptized, and said to him, "Teacher, what shall we do?"

And he said to them, "Collect no more than what is appointed for you."

In the same way, the soldiers asked him, saying, "And what shall we do?"

He said to them, "Do not intimidate anyone or accuse falsely, and be content with your wages."

Now as the people were in expectation, and all reasoned in their hearts about John, whether he was the Christ or not. John answered, saying to all, "I indeed baptize you with water; but One mightier than I is coming, whose sandal strap I am not worthy to loose. He will baptize you with the Holy Spirit and fire. His winnowing fan is in His hand, and He will thoroughly clean out His threshing floor, and gather the wheat into His barn; but the chaff He will burn with unquenchable fire." And with many other exhortations he preached to the people.

Matthew 3:13-17, Mark 1:9-11, Luke 3:21-22, John 1:29-34

John Baptizes Jesus the Lamb of God

The next day Jesus came from Nazareth of Galilee to John at the Jordan to be baptized by him. John saw Jesus coming toward him, and said, "Behold! The Lamb of God who takes away the sin of the world! This is He of whom I said, 'After me comes a Man who is preferred before me, for He was before me.' I did not know Him; but that He should be revealed to Israel, therefore I came baptizing with water."

When all the people were baptized, it came to pass that Jesus also was baptized. John tried to prevent Him, saying, "I need to be baptized by You, and are You coming to me?"

But Jesus answered and said to him, "Permit it to be so now, for thus it is fitting for us to fulfill all righteousness." Then he allowed Him.

While He prayed, the heaven was opened. When He had been baptized, Jesus came up immediately from the water, and the Holy Spirit descended in bodily form like a dove and resting upon Him, and a voice came from heaven which said, "You are My beloved Son; in You I am well pleased."

And John gave witness, saying, "I saw the Spirit descending from heaven like a dove, and He remained upon Him. I did not know Him, but He who sent me to baptize with water said to me, 'Upon whom you see the Spirit descending, and remaining on Him, this is He who baptizes with the Holy Spirit.' And I have seen and testified that this is the Son of God."

Luke 3:23-38

The Genealogy of Jesus Christ

Now Jesus Himself began His ministry at about thirty years of age, being (as was supposed) the son of Joseph, the son of Heli, the son of Matthat, the son of Levi, the son of Melchi, the son of Janna, the son of Joseph, the son of Mattathiah, the son of Amos, the son of Nahum, the son of Esli, the son of Naggai, the son of Maath, the son of Mattathiah, the son of Semei, the son of Joseph, the son of Judah, the son of Joannas, the son of Rhesa, the son of Zerubbabel, the son of Shealtiel, the son of Neri, the son of Melchi, the son of Addi, the son of Cosam, the son of Elmodam, the son of Er, the son of Jose, the son of Eliezer, the son of Jorim, the son of Matthat, the son of Levi, the son of Simeon, the son of Judah, the son of Joseph, the son of Jonan, the son of Eliakim, the son of Melea, the son of Menan, the son of Mattathah, the son of Nathan, the son of David, the son of Jesse, the son of Obed, the son of Boaz, the son of Salmon, the son of Nahshon, the son of Amminadab, the son of Ram, the son of Hezron, the son of Perez, the son of Judah, the son of Jacob, the son of Isaac, the son of Abraham, the son of Terah, the son of Nahor, the son of Serug, the son of Reu, the son of Peleg, the son of Eber, the son of Shelah, the son of Cainan, the son of Arphaxad, the son of Shem, the son of Noah, the son of Lamech, the son of Methuselah, the son of Enoch, the son of Jared, the son of Mahalalel, the son of Cainan, the son of Enosh, the son of Seth, the son of Adam, the son of God.

Matthew 4:1-11, Mark 1:12-13, Luke 4:1-13

Satan Tempts Jesus

Then Jesus was led up by the Spirit who drove Him into the wilderness to be tempted by the devil. He was there in the wilderness forty days, tempted by Satan, and was with the wild beasts. When He had fasted forty days and forty nights, having eaten nothing, afterward He was hungry.

Now when the tempter came to Jesus, he said, "If You are the Son of God, command that these stones become bread."

But He answered and said, "It is written, *'Man shall not live by bread alone, but by every word that proceeds from the mouth of God.'*"

Then the devil took Jesus up into the holy city, set Him on the pinnacle of the temple, and said to Him, "If You are the Son of God, throw Yourself down. For it is written:

'He shall give His angels charge over you,' and,
'In their hands they shall bear you up,
Lest you dash your foot against a stone.'"

Jesus said to him, "It is written again, *'You shall not tempt the Lord your God.'*"

Again, the devil took Jesus up on an exceedingly high mountain, and showed Him all the kingdoms of the world and their glory in a moment of time. And he said to Him, "All this authority I will give You, and I will give You glory; for this has been delivered to me, and I give it to whomever I wish. Therefore, if You will fall down and worship me, all will be Yours."

Then Jesus said to him, "Away with you, Satan! For it is written, *'You shall worship the Lord your God, and Him only you shall serve.'*"

When the devil had left Him, had ended every temptation, he departed from Him until an opportune time, and behold, angels came and ministered to Him.

John 1:35-40

Jesus meets Two Disciples

After the time of Jesus being instructed and tested, John stood at the river Jordan with two of his disciples. And looking at Jesus as He walked, he said, "Behold the Lamb of God!" The two disciples heard him speak, and they followed Jesus.

Then Jesus turned, and seeing them following, said to them, "What do you seek?"

They said to Him, "Rabbi" (which is to say, when translated, Teacher), "where are You staying?"

He said to them, "Come and see."

They came and saw where He was staying, and remained with Him that day (now it was about the tenth hour). One of the two who heard John speak, and followed Him, was Andrew, Simon Peter's brother.

John 1:43-51

The First Disciples. Philip and Nathaniel

The following day Jesus wanted to go to Galilee, where He found Philip and said to him, "Follow Me."

Now Philip was from Bethsaida, the city of Andrew and Peter. Philip found Nathanael and said to him, "We have found Him of whom Moses in the law, and also the prophets, wrote, Jesus of Nazareth, the son of Joseph."

Nathanael replied to him, "Can anything good come out of Nazareth?"

Philip said to him, "Come and see."

Jesus saw Nathanael coming toward Him, and said of him, "Behold, an Israelite, in whom is no deceit!"

Nathanael said to Him, "How do You know me?"

Jesus answered and said to him, "Before Philip called you, when you were under the fig tree, I saw you."

Nathanael answered and said to Him, "Rabbi, You are the Son of God! You are the King of Israel!"

Jesus answered and said to him, "Because I said to you, 'I saw you under the fig tree,' do you believe? You will see greater things than these." And He said to him, "With certainty, I tell you, hereafter you shall see heaven open, and the angels of God ascending and descending upon the Son of Man."

John 2:1-12

Water Turned to Wine

On the third day, there was a wedding in Cana of Galilee, and the mother of Jesus was there. Now both Jesus and His disciples were invited to the wedding. And when they ran out of wine, the mother of Jesus said to Him, "They have no wine."

Jesus said to her, "Woman, what does your concern have to do with Me? My hour has not yet come."

His mother said to the servants, "Whatever He says to you, do it."

Now there were set there six waterpots of stone, according to the manner of purification of the Jews, containing twenty or thirty gallons apiece. Jesus said to them, "Fill the waterpots with water." And they filled them up to the brim. And He said to them, "Draw some out now, and take it to the master of the feast." And they took it. When the master of the feast had tasted the water that was made wine, and did not know where it came from (but the servants who had drawn the water knew), the master of the feast called the bridegroom.

And he said to him, "Every man at the beginning sets out the good wine, and when the guests have well drunk, then the inferior. You have kept the good wine until now!"

These were the beginning of the signs Jesus did in Cana of Galilee, and manifested His glory; and His disciples believed in Him. After this He went down to Capernaum, He, His mother, His brothers, and His disciples, but they did not stay there many days.

John 2:13-25

Jesus Cleanses the Temple

Now the Passover of the Jews was at hand, and Jesus went up to Jerusalem. And He found in the temple those who sold oxen and sheep and doves, and the money changers doing business. When He had made a whip of cords, He drove them all out of the temple, with the sheep and the oxen, and poured out the changers' money and overturned the tables. And He said to those who sold doves, "Take these things away! Do not make My Father's house a house of merchandise!"

Then His disciples remembered that it was written, *"Zeal for Your house has eaten Me up."*

The Jews answered and said to Him, "What sign do You show to us, since You do these things?"

Jesus answered and said to them, "Destroy this temple, and in three days I will raise it up."

Then the Jews said, "It has taken forty-six years to build this temple, and will You raise it up in three days?"

But He was speaking of the temple of His body. When Jesus had risen from the dead, His disciples remembered He had said this to them; and they believed the Scripture and the word which Jesus had said.

The Discerner of Hearts

Now when Jesus was in Jerusalem at the Passover, during the feast, many believed in His name when they saw the signs which He did. But Jesus did not commit Himself to them, because He knew all men, and had no need that anyone should testify of man, for He knew what was in man.

John 3:1-36

The New Birth

There was a man of the Pharisees named Nicodemus, a ruler of the Jews. This man came to Jesus by night and said to Him, "Rabbi, we know that You are a teacher come from God; for no one can do these signs that You do unless God is with him."

Jesus answered and said to him, "I say to you, unless one is born again, he cannot see the kingdom of God."

Nicodemus said to Him, "How can a man be born when he is old? Can he enter a second time into his mother's womb and be born?"

Jesus answered, "I say to you, unless one is born of water and the Spirit, he cannot enter the kingdom of God. That which is born of the flesh is flesh, and that which is born of the Spirit is spirit. Do not marvel that I said to you, 'You must be born again.' The wind blows where it wishes, and you hear the sound of it, but cannot tell where it comes from and where it goes. So is everyone who is born of the Spirit."

Nicodemus answered and said to Him, "How can these things be?"

Jesus answered and said to him, "Are you the teacher of Israel, and do not know these things? I say to you, We speak what We know and testify what We have seen, and you do not receive Our witness. If I have told you earthly things and you do not believe, how will you believe if I tell you heavenly things? No one has ascended to heaven but He who came down from heaven, that is, the Son of Man who is in heaven. And as Moses lifted up the serpent in the wilderness, even so must the Son of Man be lifted up, that whoever believes in Him should not perish but have eternal life. For God so loved the world that He gave His only begotten Son, that whoever believes in Him should not perish but have everlasting life. For God did not send His Son into the world to condemn the world, but that the world through Him might be saved.

"He who believes in Him is not condemned; but he who does not believe is condemned already, because he has not believed in the name of the only begotten Son of God. And this is the condemnation, that the light has come into the world, and men loved darkness rather than light, because their deeds were evil. For everyone practicing evil hates the light and does not come to the light, lest his deeds should be exposed. But he who does the truth comes to the light, that his deeds may be clearly seen, that they have been done in God."

John the Baptist Exalts Christ

After these things Jesus and His disciples came into the land of Judea, and there He remained with them and baptized. Now John also was baptizing in Aenon near Salim, because there was much water there. And many came and were baptized, for John had not yet been thrown into prison.

Then there arose a dispute between some of John's disciples and the Jews about purification. And they came to John and said to him, "Rabbi, He who was with you beyond the Jordan, to whom you have testified, observe. He is baptizing, and all are coming to Him!"

John answered and said, "A man can receive nothing unless it has been given to him from heaven. You yourselves bear me witness, that I said, 'I am not the Christ,' but, 'I have been sent before Him.' He who has the bride is the bridegroom; but the friend of the bridegroom, who stands and hears him, rejoices greatly because of the bridegroom's voice. For this reason, this joy of mine is fulfilled. He must increase, but I must decrease. He who comes from above is above all; he who is of the earth is earthly and speaks of the earth. He who comes from heaven is above all. And what He has seen and heard, that He testifies; and no one receives His testimony. He who has received His testimony has certified that God is true. For He whom God has sent speaks the words of God, for God does not give the Spirit by measure. The Father loves the Son, and has given all things into His hand. He who believes in the Son has everlasting life; and he who does not believe the Son shall not see life, but the wrath of God abides on him."

Luke 3:19-20

John the Baptist Imprisoned

Herod the tetrarch, being rebuked by John concerning Herodias, his brother Philip's wife, and for all the evils which Herod had done, locked John up in prison.

John 4:1-45

A Samaritan Woman Meets Her Messiah

Therefore, when the Lord knew that the Pharisees had heard that Jesus made and baptized more disciples than John (though Jesus Himself did not baptize, but His disciples), He left Judea and departed again to Galilee. But He needed to go through Samaria.

Jesus came to a city of Samaria, which is called Sychar, near the plot of ground that Jacob gave to his son Joseph. Now Jacob's well was there. Jesus being wearied from His journey, sat by the well. It was about the sixth hour.

A woman of Samaria came to draw water.

Jesus said to her, "Give Me a drink." For His disciples had gone away into the city to buy food.

Then the woman of Samaria said to Him, "How is it that You, being a Jew, ask a drink from me, a Samaritan woman?" For Jews have no dealings with Samaritans.

Jesus answered and said to her, "If you knew the gift of God, and who it is who says to you, 'Give Me a drink,' you would have asked Him, and He would have given you living water."

The woman said to Him, "Sir, You have nothing to draw with, and the well is deep. Where then do You get this living water? Are You greater than our father Jacob, who gave us the well, and drank from it himself, as well as his sons and his livestock?"

Jesus answered and said to her, "Whoever drinks of this water will thirst again, but whoever drinks of the water that I shall give him will never thirst. But the water that I shall give him will become in him a fountain of water springing up into everlasting life."

The woman said to Him, "Sir, give me this water, that I may not thirst, nor come here to draw."

Jesus said to her, "Go, call your husband, and come here."

The woman answered and said, "I have no husband."

Jesus said to her, "You have said well, 'I have no husband,' for you have had five husbands, and the one whom you now have is not your husband; in that you spoke truly."

The woman said to Him, "Sir, I perceive that You are a prophet. Our fathers worshiped on this mountain, and you Jews say that in Jerusalem is the place where one should worship."

Jesus said to her, "Woman, believe Me, the hour is coming when you will neither on this mountain, or in Jerusalem, worship the Father. You worship what you do not know; we know what we worship, for salvation is of the Jews. But the hour is coming, and is here now, when the true worshipers will worship the Father in spirit and truth; for the Father is seeking such to worship Him. God is Spirit, and those who worship Him must worship in spirit and truth."

The woman said to Him, "I know that Messiah is coming" (who is called Christ). "When He comes, He will tell us all things."

Jesus said to her, "I who speak to you am He."

The Whitened Harvest

And at this point His disciples came, and they wondered why He talked with a woman; yet no one said, "What do You seek?" or, "Why are You talking with her?"

The woman then left her waterpot, went her way into the city, and said to the men, "Come, see a Man who told me all things that I ever did. Could this be the Christ?"

Then they went out of the city and came to Him.

In the meantime, His disciples urged Him, saying, "Rabbi, eat."

But He said to them, "I have food to eat of which you do not know."

Therefore, the disciples said to one another, "Has anyone brought Him anything to eat?"

Jesus said to them, "My food is to do the will of Him who sent Me, and to finish His work. Do you not say, 'There are still four months and then comes the harvest'? Behold, I say to you, lift up your eyes and look at the fields, for they are already white for harvest! And he who reaps receives wages, and gathers fruit for eternal life, that both he who sows and he who reaps may rejoice together. For in this the saying is true: 'One sows and another reaps.' I sent you to reap that for which you have not laboured; others have laboured, and you have entered into their labours."

The Saviour of the World

And many of the Samaritans of that city believed in Him because of the word of the woman who testified, "He told me all that I ever did." When the Samaritans came to Him, they urged Him to stay with them; and He stayed there two days. And many more believed because of His own word.

Then they said to the woman, "Now we believe, not because of what you said, for we ourselves have heard Him and we know that this is indeed the Christ, the Saviour of the world."

Welcome at Galilee

After two days, Jesus departed from there and went to Galilee. For Jesus, Himself testified that a prophet has no honour in his own country. When He came to Galilee, the Galileans received Him, having seen all the things He did in Jerusalem at the feast; for they also had gone to the feast.

Matthew 4:12-17, Mark 1:14-15, Luke 4:14-30

Jesus Begins His Galilean Ministry

When Jesus heard that John had been put into prison, He returned in the power of the Spirit to Galilee, preaching the gospel of the kingdom of God, and saying, "The time is fulfilled, and the kingdom of God is at hand. Repent, and believe in the gospel."

And news of Him went out through all the surrounding region. And He taught in their synagogues, being glorified by all.

Jesus Rejected at Nazareth

Jesus came to Nazareth, where He had been brought up. And as was His custom, He went into the synagogue on the Sabbath day, and stood up to read. And He was handed the book of the prophet Isaiah.

And when He had opened the book, He found the place where it was written:

"The Spirit of the Lord is upon Me,
Because He has anointed Me
To preach the gospel to the poor;
He has sent Me to heal the brokenhearted,
To proclaim liberty to the captives
And recovery of sight to the blind,
To set at liberty those who are oppressed;
To proclaim the acceptable year of the Lord."

Then He closed the book, and gave it back to the attendant and sat down. And the eyes of all who were in the synagogue were fixed on Him.

And He began to say to them, "Today this Scripture is fulfilled in your hearing."

All bore witness to Him, and marvelled at the gracious words which proceeded out of His mouth. And they said, "Is this not Joseph's son?"

He said to them, "You will surely say this proverb to Me, 'Physician, heal yourself! Whatever we have heard done in Capernaum, do also here in Your country.'" Then He said, "With certainty, I say to you, no prophet is accepted in his own country. But I tell you truly, many widows were in Israel in the days of Elijah, when the heaven was shut up three years and six months, and there was a great famine throughout all the land; but to none of them was Elijah sent except to Zarephath, in the region of Sidon, to a woman who was a widow. And many lepers were in Israel in the time of Elisha the prophet, and none of them was cleansed except Naaman the Syrian."

All those in the synagogue, when they heard these things, were filled with wrath, and rose up and thrust Him out of the city;

and they led Him to the brow of the hill on which their city was built, that they might throw Him down over the cliff. Then passing through the middle of them, He went His way.

Jesus Goes to Capernaum

Leaving Nazareth, Jesus came and dwelt in Capernaum, which is by the sea, in the regions of Zebulun and Naphtali, that it might be fulfilled which was spoken by Isaiah the prophet, saying,

"The land of Zebulun and the land of Naphtali,
By the way of the sea, beyond the Jordan, Galilee of the Gentiles.
The people who sat in darkness have seen a great light,
And upon those who sat in the region and shadow of death
Light has dawned."

From that time Jesus began to preach and to say, "Repent, for the kingdom of heaven is at hand."

Matthew 4:18-22, Mark 1:16-20, Luke 5:1-11, John 1:41-42

Four Fishermen Called as Disciples

Jesus, walking by the Sea of Galilee, saw two brothers, Simon called Peter, and Andrew his brother, casting a net into the sea; for they were fishermen.

As He stood by the Lake of Gennesaret, Jesus saw two boats moored by the lake; but the fishermen had gone from them and were washing their nets. When He had gone a little further from there, He saw two other brothers, James the son of Zebedee, and

John his brother, in the boat with Zebedee their father, mending their nets in the boat with the hired servants.

The multitude pressed about Jesus to hear the word of God. So, Jesus climbed into one of the boats, which was Simon's, and asked him to put out a little from the land. Jesus sat down and taught the multitudes from the boat. When He had stopped speaking, He said to Simon, "Launch out into the deep and let down your nets for a catch."

But Simon answered and said to Him, "Master, we have toiled all night and caught nothing; nevertheless, at Your word I will let down the net."

And when they had done this, they caught a great number of fish, and their net was breaking. They signalled to their partners in the other boat to come and help them. And they came and filled both the boats, so that they began to sink.

When Simon Peter saw it, he fell down at Jesus' knees, saying, "Depart from me, for I am a sinful man, O Lord!" And Peter returned to the fish and the nets in the boat.

For he and all who were with him were astonished at the catch of fish which they had taken; and so also were James and John, the sons of Zebedee, who were partners with Simon.

Andrew turned to his brother Simon, and said to him, "We have found the Messiah" (which is translated, the Christ). And together they turned and looked at Jesus.

Now when Jesus looked at him, He said, "You are Simon the son of Jonah. You shall be called Cephas" (which is translated, A Stone). And Jesus said to Simon and Andrew, "Do not be afraid. Follow Me, and I will make you become fishers of men. From now on you will catch men."

When they had brought their boats to land, they immediately left their nets, forsook all and followed Him.

When Jesus had gone a little further from there, He saw two other brothers, James the son of Zebedee, and John his brother, in the boat with Zebedee their father. He called them, and immediately they left the boat and their father Zebedee in the boat with the hired servants, and followed Him.

Mark 1:21-28, Luke 4:31-37

Jesus Casts Out an Unclean Spirit

Then Jesus, and His six disciples went into Capernaum, a city of Galilee and immediately on the Sabbath He entered the synagogue and taught. And they were astonished at His teaching, for He taught them as one having authority, and not as the scribes.

Now there was a man in their synagogue who had a spirit of an unclean demon.

And he cried out, saying, "Let us alone! What have we to do with You, Jesus of Nazareth? Did You come to destroy us? I know who You are, the Holy One of God!"

But Jesus rebuked him, saying, "Be quiet, and come out of him!"

And when the unclean spirit had convulsed him, thrown him in their midst, and cried out with a loud voice, it came out of him and did not hurt him.

Then they were all amazed, so that they questioned and spoke among themselves, saying, "What a word is this! What new doctrine is this? For with authority and power He commands even the unclean spirits, and they obey Him and come out."

And immediately the report about Him went out. His fame spread throughout all the region, into every place in the surrounding area around Galilee.

Matthew 8:14-17, Mark 1:29-34, Luke 4:38-41

Peter's Mother-in-Law Healed

As soon as Jesus and His disciples came out of the synagogue, they entered the house of Simon and Andrew, with James and John. But Simon's wife's mother lay sick with a fever, and they told Him about her at once, and made a request of Him. Jesus came and took her by the hand and lifted her up, and immediately the fever left her. And she served them.

Many Healed in the Evening after Sabbath Sunset

When the sun had set and evening had come, the people of Capernaum, brought to Jesus all who were sick, and many who were demon-possessed. The whole city was gathered together at the door. He laid His hands on every one of them. Jesus healed many who were sick with various diseases, and cast out many demons; many came out crying, saying, "You are the Christ, the Son of God!"

And He, rebuking them, did not allow them to speak, for they knew that He was the Christ. And Jesus cast out the spirits with a word, and healed all who were sick, that it might be fulfilled which was spoken by Isaiah the prophet, saying:

*"He Himself took our infirmities
And bore our sickness."*

Matthew 4:23-25, Mark 1:35-39, Luke 4:42-44

Jesus Heals a Great Multitude

Jesus went about all Galilee, teaching in their synagogues, preaching the gospel of the kingdom, and healing all kinds of sickness and all kinds of disease among the people. Then His fame went throughout all Syria; and they brought to Him all sick people who were afflicted with various diseases and torments, and those who were demon-possessed, epileptics, and paralytics; and He healed them. Great multitudes followed Him from Galilee, Decapolis, Jerusalem, Judea, and beyond the Jordan.

Jesus Preaches in Galilee

In the morning, having risen a long while before daylight, Jesus went out and departed to a deserted, solitary place; and there He prayed. And Simon and those who were with Him searched for Him. When they found Him, they said to Him, "Everyone is looking for You."

But He said to them, "Let us go into the next towns, that I may preach there also, because this purpose is what I came for."

And the crowd sought Him and came to Him, and tried to keep Him from leaving them; but He said to them, "I must preach the kingdom of God to the other cities also, because for this purpose I have been sent."

And He was preaching in their synagogues throughout all Galilee, and casting out demons.

Matthew 8:1-4, Mark 1:40-45, Luke 5:12-16

Jesus Cleanses a Leper

And it happened, when Jesus was in a certain city, a man who was full of leprosy saw Jesus and came to Him, imploring Him, kneeling down before Him and saying to Him, "If You are willing, You can make me clean."

Then Jesus, moved with compassion, stretched out His hand and touched him, and said to him, "I am willing; be cleansed."

As soon as Jesus had spoken, immediately the leprosy left him, and he was cleansed. And Jesus strictly warned him and sent him away at once, and said to him, "See that you say nothing to anyone; but go your way, show yourself to the priest, and offer for your cleansing those things which Moses commanded, as a testimony to them."

However, he went out and began to proclaim it freely, and to spread the matter, so that Jesus could no longer openly enter the city, but was outside in deserted places; and they came to Him from every direction. Great multitudes came together to hear, and to be healed by Him of their infirmities.

Jesus Himself often withdrew into the wilderness and prayed.

Matthew 9:1-17, Mark 2:1-22, Luke 5:17-39

Jesus Forgives and Heals a Paralytic

Jesus got into a boat, crossed over, and entered Capernaum after some days, and came to His own city. It was heard that He was in the house. Immediately many gathered together, so that there was no longer room to receive them, not even near the door. And He preached the word to them.

Now it happened on this certain day, as He was teaching, there were Pharisees and teachers of the law sitting by, who had come out of every town of Galilee, Judea, and Jerusalem. And the power of the Lord was present to heal. Then some men brought a man who was paralyzed on a bed, whom they wanted to bring in and lay before Him. And when they could not find a way in, because of the crowd, they went up onto the housetop. When they had broken through the tiling, they let down the bed on which the paralytic was lying into the midst before Jesus.

When Jesus saw their faith, He said to the paralytic, "Son, be of good cheer; your sins are forgiven you."

And some of the scribes were sitting there and reasoning in their hearts, "Why does this Man speak blasphemies like this? Who can forgive sins but God alone? This Man blasphemes!"

But immediately, Jesus perceived in His spirit they reasoned this way within themselves. Jesus said to them, "Why do you reason about these things in your hearts? Why do you think evil in your hearts? For which is easier to say, 'Your sins are forgiven you,' or to say, 'Arise, take up your bed and walk? But that you may know that the Son of Man has power on earth to forgive sins,' He said to the paralytic, 'Arise, take up your bed, and go to your house.'"

Immediately he arose, took up the bed, and went out in the presence of them all, and departed to his house, glorifying God.

Now when the multitudes saw it, they marvelled and glorified God, saying, "We have never seen anything like this! Who has given such power to this man?" And they were all amazed, and they glorified God and were filled with fear, saying, "We have seen strange things today!"

Matthew the Tax Collector

Jesus went out again by the sea, all the multitude came to Him, and He taught them. As Jesus passed on from there, He saw a man named Matthew (Levi the son of Alphaeus) sitting at the tax office. Jesus said to him, "Follow Me." So, he left all, arose and followed Him.

Now it happened, Matthew gave Him a great feast in his own house. As Jesus sat at the table, many tax collectors and sinners came and sat down with Jesus and His disciples, for they were many, and they followed Him. And when the scribes and Pharisees saw Him eating with the tax collectors and sinners, they complained to His disciples, saying, "Why does your Teacher eat and drink with tax collectors and sinners?"

When Jesus heard this, He said to them, "Those who are well have no need of a physician, but those who are sick. But go and learn what this means: 'I desire mercy and not sacrifice.' For I did not come to call the righteous, but sinners, to repentance."

Jesus Is Questioned About Fasting

The disciples of John and of the Pharisees were fasting. Then the disciples of John came to Jesus and said, "Why do we fast often and make prayers, and likewise those of the Pharisees, but Your disciples eat and drink and do not fast?"

And Jesus said to them, "Can the friends of the bridegroom fast while the bridegroom is with them? As long as they have the bridegroom with them they cannot fast. But the days will come when the bridegroom will be taken away from them, and then they will fast in those days."

Then He spoke a parable to them. "No one sews a piece of unshrunk cloth on an old garment; or else the new piece pulls away from the old, and the tear is made worse. And no one puts new wine into old wineskins; or else the new wine bursts the wineskins, the wine is spilled, and the wineskins are ruined. But new wine must be put into new wineskins, and both are preserved. No one, having drunk old wine, immediately desires new; for he says, 'The old is better.'"

Matthew 12:1-14, Mark 2:23 to 3:6, Luke 6:1-11

Jesus Is Lord of the Sabbath

Now it happened, Jesus went through the grainfields on the second Sabbath after the first. And His disciples were hungry, and as they went they began to pluck heads of grain, rubbing them in their hands to eat. And when the Pharisees saw it, they said to Him, "Look, Your disciples are doing what is not lawful to do on the Sabbath!"

But He said to them, "Have you not read what David did when he was in need and hungry, he and those who were with him: how he entered the house of God in the days of Abiathar the high priest, and ate the showbread, which was not lawful for him to eat, nor for those who were with him, but only for the priests? Or have you not read in the law that on the Sabbath the priests in the temple profane the Sabbath, and are blameless? Yet I say to you that in this place there is One greater than the temple. But if you had known what this means, *'I desire mercy and not sacrifice,'* you would not have condemned the guiltless." And He said to them, "The Sabbath was made for man, and not man for the Sabbath. Therefore, the Son of Man is also Lord of the Sabbath."

Healing on the Sabbath

Now when Jesus had departed from there, He entered the synagogue again, on another Sabbath and taught. And a man was there who had a withered right hand. So, the scribes and Pharisees watched Him closely, whether He would heal him on the Sabbath, so that they might accuse Him.

But He knew their thoughts, and He said to the man who had the withered hand, "Arise. Step forward and stand here." And he arose and stood.

Then Jesus said to them, "I will ask you one thing: Is it lawful on the Sabbath to do good or to do evil, to save life or to destroy?" But they kept silent.

And when He had looked around at them with anger, being grieved by the hardness of their hearts, He said to the man, "Stretch out your hand." And he stretched it out, and his hand was restored as whole as the other.

Then the Pharisees were filled with rage, went out and immediately plotted with the Herodians against Him, how they might destroy Jesus.

Matthew 12:15-21, Mark 3:7-19, Luke 6:12-19

Behold, My Servant

But when Jesus knew the Pharisees were angry, He withdrew from there, with a great multitude following Him, and He healed them all. Yet He warned them not to make Him known, that it might be fulfilled which was spoken by Isaiah the prophet, saying:

"Behold! My Servant whom I have chosen,
My Beloved in whom My soul is well pleased!
I will put My Spirit upon Him,
And He will declare justice to the Gentiles.
He will not quarrel nor cry out,
Nor will anyone hear His voice in the streets.
A bruised reed He will not break,
And smoking flax He will not quench,
Till He sends forth justice to victory;
And in His Name Gentiles will trust."

A Great Multitude Follows Jesus

Then Jesus withdrew with His disciples to the sea. And a great multitude from Galilee followed Him, and from Judea, Jerusalem and Idumea and beyond the Jordan; and those from Tyre and Sidon when they heard how many things He was doing, came to Him. So, He told His disciples that a small boat should be kept ready for Him because of the multitude. Jesus was concerned these people might crush Him. He healed many, so that those who had afflictions pushed toward Him, so they might just touch Him. And the unclean spirits, whenever they saw Him, fell down before Him and cried out, saying, "You are the Son of God." But He sternly warned them that they should not make Him known.

Jesus Heals a Great Multitude

And Jesus came away from where He was healing, and stood on a level place with a crowd of His disciples and a great multitude of people from all Judea and Jerusalem, and from the seacoast of Tyre and Sidon. These people came to hear Jesus and be healed of their diseases, as well as those who were tormented with unclean spirits. And they were all healed. And the whole multitude sought to touch Him, for power went out from Him and healed them all.

The Twelve Apostles

Now it happened in those days, that Jesus went out to the mountain to pray, and called to Himself those He had chosen. Jesus continued all night in prayer to God. And when it was day, He called His disciples, and from them He chose twelve, whom He also named apostles that they might be with Him and that He might send them out to preach, and to have power to heal sicknesses, and to cast out demons. Simon, to whom He gave the name Peter, James the son of Zebedee and John the brother of James, to whom He gave the name Boanerges, that is, "Sons of Thunder"; Andrew, Philip, Bartholomew, Matthew, Thomas, James the son of Alphaeus, Thaddaeus, Simon the Cananite; and Judas Iscariot, who also betrayed Him. And they went into a house.

Matthew 5:1-48, Luke 6:20-36

The Beatitudes

And seeing the multitudes, Jesus went up on a mountain, and when He was seated His disciples came to Him. Then He opened His mouth and taught them, saying:

"Blessed are the poor in spirit, for theirs is the kingdom of heaven.
Blessed are those who mourn, for they shall be comforted.
Blessed are the meek, for they shall inherit the earth.
Blessed are those who hunger and thirst for righteousness, for they shall be filled.
Blessed are the merciful, for they shall obtain mercy.
Blessed are the pure in heart, for they shall see God.
Blessed are the peacemakers, for they shall be called sons of God.
Blessed are those who are persecuted for righteousness' sake, for theirs is the kingdom of heaven.
Blessed are you when they revile and persecute you, and say all kinds of evil against you falsely for My sake.
Rejoice and be exceedingly glad, for great is your reward in heaven, for so they persecuted the prophets who were before you."

Jesus Pronounces Woes

"But woe to you who are rich, for you have received your consolation.
Woe to you who are full, for you shall hunger.
Woe to you who laugh now, for you shall mourn and weep.
Woe to you when all men speak well of you, for so did their
fathers to the false prophets."

Believers Are Salt and Light

"You are the salt of the earth; but if the salt loses its flavour, how
shall it be seasoned? It is then good for nothing but to be thrown
out and trampled underfoot by men.

"You are the light of the world. A city that is set on a hill cannot
be hidden. Those in the house, do not light a lamp and put it under
a basket, but on a lampstand, and it gives light to all who are in the
house. Let your light so shine before men, that they may see your
good works and glorify your Father in heaven.

Christ Fulfils the Law

"Do not think that I came to destroy the Law or the Prophets? I
did not come to destroy but to fulfill. I say to you, till heaven and
earth pass away, one jot or one tittle will by no means pass from
the law till all is fulfilled. Whoever therefore breaks one of the
least of these commandments, and teaches men so, shall be called
least in the kingdom of heaven; but whoever does and teaches
them, he shall be called great in the kingdom of heaven. For I
say to you, that unless your righteousness exceeds the righteousness of the scribes and Pharisees, you will by no means enter the
kingdom of heaven.

Murder Begins in the Heart

"You have heard that it was said to those of old, *'You shall not murder,* and whoever murders will be in danger of the judgment.' But I say to you that whoever is angry with his brother without a cause shall be in danger of the judgment. And whoever says to his brother, 'Raca!' shall be in danger of the council. But whoever says, 'You fool!' shall be in danger of hell fire. If you bring your gift to the altar, and there remember that your brother has something against you, leave your gift there before the altar, and go your way. First be reconciled to your brother, and then come and offer your gift. Agree with your enemy quickly, while you are on the way with him, before your enemy delivers you to the judge, and the judge hand you over to the officer, and you be thrown into prison. I say to you, you will by no means get out of there until you have paid the full amount.

Adultery in the Heart

"You have heard that it was said to those of old, *'You shall not commit adultery.'* But I say to you, whoever looks at a woman to lust for her has already committed adultery with her in his heart. If your right eye causes you to sin, pluck it out and cast it from you; for it is more profitable for you that one of your members perish, than for your whole body to be thrown into hell. And if your right hand causes you to sin, cut it off and cast it from you; for it is more profitable for you that one of your members perish, than for your whole body to be thrown into hell.

Marriage Is Sacred and Binding

"It has been said, 'Whoever divorces his wife, let him give her a certificate of divorce.' But I say to you that whoever divorces his wife for any reason except sexual immorality, causes her to commit adultery; and whoever marries a woman who is divorced, commits adultery.

Jesus Forbids Oaths

"Again, you have heard it said to those of old, 'You shall not swear falsely, but shall perform your oaths to the Lord.' But I say to you, do not swear at all: neither by heaven, for it is God's throne; nor by the earth, for it is His footstool; nor by Jerusalem, for it is the city of the great King. Nor shall you swear by your head, because you cannot make one hair white or black. But let your 'Yes' be 'Yes,' and your 'No,' 'No.' For whatever is more than these is from the evil one.

Go the Second Mile

"You have heard it said, *'An eye for an eye and a tooth for a tooth.'* But I tell you not to resist an evil person. Whoever slaps you on your right cheek, turn the other to him also. If anyone wants to sue you and take away your tunic, let him have your cloak also. And whoever compels you to go one mile, go with him two. Give to him who asks you, and from him who wants to borrow from you, do not turn away.

Love Your Enemies

"You have heard it said, *'You shall love your neighbour* and hate your enemy.' But I say to you, love your enemies, bless those who curse you, do good to those who hate you, and pray for those who spitefully use you and persecute you, that you may be sons of your Father in heaven; for He makes His sun rise on the evil and on the good, and sends rain on the just and on the unjust. For if you love those who love you, what reward have you? Do not even the tax collectors do the same? And if you greet your brethren only, what do you do more than others? Do not even the tax collectors do this? You should try to be perfect, just as your Father in heaven is perfect. To him who strikes you on the one cheek, offer the other also. And from him who takes away your cloak, do not withhold your tunic either. Give to everyone who asks of you. And from him who takes away your goods do not ask them back. And just as you would want men to do to you, you also do the same to them.

But if you love those who love you, what credit is that to you? For even sinners love those who love them. And if you do good to those who do good to you, what credit is that to you? For even sinners do the same. And if you lend to those from whom you hope to receive back, what credit is that to you? For even sinners lend to sinners to receive as much back. But love your enemies, do good, and lend, hoping for nothing in return; and your reward will be great, and you will be sons of the Most High. For He is kind to the unthankful and evil. Therefore, be merciful, just as your Father also is merciful.

Matthew 6:1-34, Luke 11:1-4, Luke 12:22-34

Do Good to Please God

"Make sure you do not do your charitable deeds before men, to be seen by them. Otherwise you have no reward from your Father in heaven. When you do a charitable deed, do not sound a trumpet before you as the hypocrites do in the synagogues and in the streets, that they may have glory from men. I say to you, they have their reward. But when you do a charitable deed, do not let your left hand know what your right hand is doing, that your charitable deed may be in secret; and your Father who sees in secret will Himself reward you openly."

The Model Prayer

Now it happened, as Jesus was praying in a certain place, when He had finished, one of His disciples said to Him, "Lord, teach us to pray, as John also taught his disciples."

Jesus said to them, "When you pray, you shall not be like the hypocrites. For they love to pray standing in the synagogues and on the corners of the streets, that they may be seen by men. I can confidently say to you, they have their reward. But you, when you pray, go into your room, and when you have shut your door, pray to your Father who is in the secret place; and your Father who sees in secret will reward you openly. And when you pray, do not use vain repetitions as the heathen do. For they think that they will be heard for their many words. I say again, do not be like them. For your Father knows the things you have need of before you ask Him. When you pray, use this as your guide:

Our Father in heaven,
Hallowed be Your name.
Your kingdom come.
Your will be done
On earth as it is in heaven.
Give us this day our daily bread.
And forgive us our sins, our debts,
As we also forgive everyone who is indebted to us.
And do not lead us into temptation,
But deliver us from the evil one.
For Yours is the kingdom and the power and the glory forever.
Amen.

"For if you forgive men their offences against you, your heavenly Father will also forgive your offences to Him. But if you do not forgive men their offences committed against you, neither will your Father forgive your offences."

Fasting to Be Seen Only by God

Jesus continued, "When you fast, do not be like the hypocrites, with a sad countenance. For they disfigure their faces that they may appear to men to be fasting. I say to you, they have their reward. But you, when you fast, anoint your head and wash your face, so that you do not appear to men to be fasting, but to your Father who is in the secret place; and your Father who sees in secret will reward you openly.

Lay Up Treasures in Heaven

"Do not lay up for yourselves treasures on earth, where moth and rust destroys and where thieves break in and steal; but lay up for yourselves treasures in heaven, where neither moth nor rust destroys and where thieves do not break in and steal. For where your treasure is, there your heart will be also.

The Lamp of the Body

"The lamp of the body is the eye. If your eye is good, your whole body will be full of light. But if your eye is bad, your whole body will be full of darkness. If the light that is in you is darkness, how great is that darkness!

You Cannot Serve God and Riches

"No one can serve two masters; for either he will hate the one and love the other, or else he will be loyal to the one and despise the other. You cannot serve God and mammon."

Do Not Worry

Then Jesus said to His disciples, "I say to you, do not worry about your life, what you will eat or what you will drink; or about the body, what you will put on. Is not life more than food, and the body is more than clothing? Look at the birds of the air. Consider the ravens, for they neither sow nor reap, which have neither storehouse nor barn; yet your heavenly Father feeds them. Of how much more value are you than the birds? And which of you by worrying can add one cubit to his stature?

"So why do you worry about clothing? If you then are not able to do the least, why are you anxious for the rest? Consider the lilies, how they grow: they neither toil nor spin; and yet I say to you, even Solomon in all his glory was not arrayed like one of these. Now if God so clothes the grass of the field, which today is in the field and tomorrow is thrown into the oven, how much more will He clothe you, O you of little faith?

"And do not seek what you should eat or what you should drink, or have an anxious mind. For all these things, the nations of the world seek after, and your Father knows that you need these things. But seek the kingdom of God and His righteousness, and all these things shall be added to you. Do not fear, little flock, for it is your Father's good pleasure to give you the kingdom. Sell what you have and give alms; provide yourselves money bags which do not grow old, a treasure in the heavens that does not fail, where no thief approaches or moth destroys. For where your treasure is, there your heart will be also. Therefore, do not worry about tomorrow, for tomorrow will worry about its own things. Sufficient for the day is its own trouble.

Matthew 7:1-29, Luke 6:37-49, Luke 11:5-13

Do Not Judge

"Judge not, and you shall not be judged. Condemn not, and you shall not be condemned. Forgive, and you will be forgiven. Give, and it will be given back to you with the measure you use: good measure, pressed down, shaken together, and running over will be put into your lap. For with the same measure that you use, it will be measured back to you."

And He spoke a parable to them: "Can the blind lead the blind? Will they not both fall into the ditch? A disciple is not above his teacher, but everyone who is perfectly trained will be like his teacher. And why do you look at the speck in your brother's eye, but do not perceive, consider the plank in your own eye? Or how can you say to your brother, 'Brother, let me remove the speck that is in your eye,' when you yourself do not see the plank that is in your own eye? Hypocrite! First remove the plank from your own eye, and then you will see clearly to remove the speck that is in your brother's eye.

"Do not give what is holy to the dogs; nor cast your pearls before swine, lest they trample them under their feet, and turn and tear you in pieces.

Keep Asking, Seeking, Knocking

"So, I say to you, ask, and it will be given to you; seek, and you will find; knock, and it will be opened to you. For everyone who asks receives, and he who seeks finds, and to him who knocks it will be opened. If a son asks for bread from any father among you, will he give him a stone? Or if he asks for a fish, will he give him a serpent instead of a fish? Or if he asks for an egg, will he offer him a scorpion? If you then, being evil, know how to give good gifts to your children, how much more will your heavenly Father give good things and the Holy Spirit to those who ask Him! Therefore, whatever you want men to do to you, do also to them, for this is the Law and the Prophets.

The Narrow Way

"Enter by the narrow gate; for wide is the gate and broad is the way that leads to destruction, and there are many who go in by it. Because narrow is the gate and difficult is the way which leads to life, and there are few who find it.

You Will Know Them by Their Fruits

"Beware of false prophets, who come to you in sheep's clothing, but inwardly they are ravenous wolves. You will know them by their fruits. For a good tree does not bear bad fruit, nor does a bad tree bear good fruit. For every tree is known by its own fruit. Do men gather grapes from thorn bushes or figs from thistles? Even so, every good tree bears good fruit, but a bad tree bears bad fruit. Every tree that does not bear good fruit is cut down and thrown into the fire. A good man out of the good treasure of his heart brings forth good; and an evil man out of the evil treasure of his heart brings forth evil. For out of the abundance of the heart his mouth speaks. Therefore, by their fruits you will know them.

I Never Knew You

"Not everyone who says to Me, 'Lord, Lord,' shall enter the kingdom of heaven, but he who does the will of My Father in heaven. Many will say to Me in that day, 'Lord, Lord, have we not prophesied in Your name, cast out demons in Your name, and done many wonders in Your name?' And then I will declare to them, 'I never knew you; depart from Me, you who practice lawlessness!'

Build on the Rock

"But why do you call Me 'Lord, Lord,' and not do the things which I say? Whoever comes to Me, and hears these sayings of Mine and does them, I will show you whom he is like. He is like a wise man building a house, who dug deep and laid the foundation on the rock. And when the flood arose, the stream beat violently against that house, and could not move it, for it was founded on the rock. But he who heard and did nothing is like a foolish man who built a house on the earth or sand without a foundation, against which the winds blew, and the stream beat violently; and immediately it fell. And the ruin of that house was great."

And so, it was, when Jesus had ended these sayings, that the people were astonished at His teaching, for He taught them as one having authority, and not as the scribes.

A Friend Comes at Midnight

And Jesus said to them, "Which of you shall have a friend, and go to him at midnight and say to him, 'Friend, lend me three loaves; for a friend of mine has come to me on his journey, and I have nothing to set before him'; and he will answer from within and say, 'Do not trouble me; the door is now shut, and my children are with me in bed; I cannot get up and give to you'? I say to you, though he will not get up and give to him because he is his friend, yet because of his persistence he will get up and give him as much as he needs."

Matthew 8:5-13, Luke 7:1-17, John 4:46-54

Jesus Heals a Centurion's Servant

When Jesus concluded all His sayings in the hearing of the people, He entered Capernaum.

A certain centurion's servant, who was dear to him, was sick and ready to die. When he heard about Jesus, he sent elders of the Jews to Him, pleading with Him to come and heal his servant. When the elders of the Jews came to Jesus, they begged Him earnestly, saying that the one for whom He should do this was deserving, "for he loves our nation, and has built us a synagogue."

And Jesus said to them, "I will come and heal him."

Now Jesus went with them. And when He was not far from the house, the centurion sent friends to Him, saying, "Lord, do not trouble Yourself, for I am not worthy that You should enter under my roof. Therefore, I did not even think myself worthy to come to You. But say the word, and my servant will be healed. For I also am a man placed under authority, having soldiers under me. And I say to one, 'Go,' and he goes; and to another, 'Come,' and he comes; and to my servant, 'Do this,' and he does it."

When Jesus heard these things, He marvelled at him, and turned around and said to the crowd that followed Him, "I say to you, I have not found such great faith, not even in Israel! And I say to you that many will come from east and west, and sit down with Abraham, Isaac, and Jacob in the kingdom of heaven. But the sons of the kingdom will be cast out into outer darkness. There will be weeping and gnashing of teeth." Then Jesus said to the friends of the centurion, "Go your way; and as you have believed, so let it be done for you."

And those who were sent, returning to the house, found the servant who had been sick, was healed that same hour.

Jesus Raises the Son of the Widow of Nain

Now it happened, the day after, Jesus went into a city called Nain; and many of His disciples, and a large crowd went with Him. And when He came near the gate of the city, behold, a dead man was being carried out, the only son of his mother; and she was a widow. And a large crowd from the city was with her.

When the Lord saw her, He had compassion on her and said to her, "Do not weep."

Then He came and touched the open coffin, and those who carried him stood still.

And He said, "Young man, I say to you, awake."

So, he who was dead sat up and began to speak. And He presented him to his mother.

Then fear came upon all, and they glorified God, saying, "A great prophet has risen up among us"; and, "God has visited His people." And this report about Him went throughout all Judea and all the surrounding region.

A Nobleman's Son Healed

Jesus came again to Cana of Galilee where He had made the water wine. And there was a certain nobleman whose son was sick at Capernaum. When he heard that Jesus had come out of Judea into Galilee, he went to Him and begged Him to come down and heal his son, for he was at the point of death.

Then Jesus said to him, "Unless you people see signs and wonders, you will by no means believe."

The nobleman said to Him, "Sir, come down before my child dies!"

Jesus said to him, "Go your way; your son lives."

So, the man believed the word that Jesus spoke to him, and he went his way. And as he was returning to his home, his servants met him and told him, saying, "Your son lives!"

Then he inquired of them the hour when he got better.

And they said to him, "Yesterday at the seventh hour the fever left him."

The father knew that it was at the same hour in which Jesus said to him, "Your son lives." And he himself believed, and his whole household.

This again is the second sign Jesus did when He had come out of Judea into Galilee.

Matthew 11:2-19, Luke 7:18-35

John the Baptist Sends Messengers to Jesus

On another occasion, when Jesus finished teaching and sharing with His twelve disciples, He departed from Cana of Galilee to teach and to preach in their cities. And when John had heard in prison about the works of Christ, he sent two of his disciples to ask Him, "Are You the Coming One, or do we look for another?"

When the men came to Jesus, they said, "John the Baptist has sent us to You, saying, 'Are You the Coming One, or do we look for another?'" That very hour Jesus cured many of infirmities, afflictions, and evil spirits; and to many blind He gave sight.

Jesus answered and said to them, "Go and tell John the things you have seen and heard: that the blind see, the lame walk, the lepers are cleansed, the deaf hear, the dead are raised, the poor have the gospel preached to them. And blessed is he who is not offended because of Me."

Then the disciples of John reported to him concerning all these things. As they departed, Jesus began to say to the multitudes concerning John: "What did you go out into the wilderness to see? A reed shaken by the wind? But what did you go out to see? A man clothed in soft garments? Indeed, those who are gorgeously apparelled and live in luxury are in kings' courts? Those who wear soft clothing are in kings' houses. But what did you go out into the wilderness to see? A prophet? Yes, I say to you, and more than a prophet. For this is he of whom it is written:

'Behold, I send My messenger before Your face,
Who will prepare Your way before You.'

"I say to you, among those born of women, there was not one born a greater prophet than John the Baptist; but he who is least in the kingdom of heaven is greater than he. And from the days of John the Baptist until now, the kingdom of heaven suffers violence, and the violent take it by force. For all the prophets and the law prophesied until John. And if you are willing to receive his word, he is Elijah who is to come. He who has ears to hear, let him hear!"

And when all the people heard Jesus, even the tax collectors justified God, having been baptized with the baptism of John. But the Pharisees and lawyers rejected the will of God for themselves, not having been baptized by him.

"But to what shall I liken this generation? It is like children sitting in the marketplaces and calling to their companions, and saying:

'We played the flute for you,
And you did not dance;
We mourned for you,
And you did not weep.'

For John the Baptist came neither eating nor drinking wine, and you say, 'He has a demon.' The Son of Man has come eating and drinking, and you say, 'Look, a glutton and a winebibber, a friend of tax collectors and sinners!' But wisdom is justified by all her children."

Luke 7:36-50

A Sinful Woman Forgiven

Then one of the Pharisees asked Jesus to eat with him. And He went to the Pharisee's house, and sat down to eat. There was a woman in the city who was a sinner. When she knew that Jesus sat at the table in the Pharisee's house, she brought an alabaster flask of fragrant oil, and sat at His feet behind Him weeping; and she began to wash His feet with her tears, and wiped them with the hair of her head; and she kissed His feet and anointed them with the fragrant oil. Now when the Pharisee who had invited Him saw this, he spoke to himself, saying, "This Man, if He were a prophet, would know who and what manner of woman this is who is touching Him, for she is a sinner."

And Jesus answered and said to him, "Simon, I have something to say to you."

He said, "Teacher, say it."

"There was a certain creditor who had two debtors. One owed five hundred denarii, and the other fifty. And when they had nothing with which to repay, he freely forgave them both. Tell Me, therefore, which of them will love him more?"

Simon answered and said, "I suppose the one whom he forgave more."

And He said to him, "You have rightly judged."

Then He turned to the woman and said to Simon, "Do you see this woman? I entered your house; you gave Me no water for My feet, but she has washed My feet with her tears and wiped them with the hair of her head. You gave Me no kiss, but this woman has not ceased to kiss My feet since the time I came in. You did not anoint My head with oil, but this woman has anointed My feet with fragrant oil. I say to you, her sins, which are many, are forgiven, for she loved much. But to whom little is forgiven, the same loves little."

Then He said to her, "Your sins are forgiven."

And those who sat at the table with Him began to say to themselves, "Who is this who even forgives sins?"

Then He said to the woman, "Your faith has saved you. Go in peace."

Matthew 12:22-50, Mark 3:20-35, Luke 11:14-36, Luke 8:19-21

A House Divided Cannot Stand

Then the multitude came together again, so that they could not so much as eat bread. Then one was brought to Jesus who was demon-possessed, blind and mute; and He healed him, so that the blind and mute man both spoke and saw. And all the multitudes were amazed and said, "Could this be the Son of David?"

When the Pharisees heard about this, they went out to lay hold of Him, for they said, "He is out of His mind." And the scribes who came down from Jerusalem said, "He has Beelzebub," and, "By the ruler of the demons He casts out demons."

But Jesus knew their thoughts, and called them to Himself and said to them, "If I cast out demons by Beelzebub, by whom do your sons cast them out? They will be your judges. How can Satan cast out Satan? If a kingdom is divided against itself, that kingdom cannot stand, it is bought to desolation, and every city or house divided against itself will not stand. If Satan casts out Satan, he is divided against himself. How then will his kingdom stand? If Satan has risen up against himself, and is divided, he cannot stand, but has an end." And Jesus spoke to them a parable. "No one can enter a strong man's house and plunder his goods, unless he first binds the strong man. But if I cast out demons by the Spirit of God, surely the kingdom of God has come upon you. He who is not with Me is against Me, and he who does not gather with Me scatters abroad.

The Unpardonable Sin

"For this reason, I say to you, every sin and blasphemy will be forgiven the sons of men, and whatever blasphemies they may utter; but he who blasphemes against the Holy Spirit never has forgiveness, but is subject to eternal condemnation. The blasphemy against the Spirit will not be forgiven men. Anyone who speaks a word against the Son of Man, it will be forgiven him; but whoever speaks against the Holy Spirit, it will not be forgiven him, either in this age or in the age to come, because they said, 'He has an unclean spirit.'

A Tree Known by Its Fruit

"Either make the tree good and its fruit good, or else make the tree bad and its fruit bad; for a tree is known by its fruit. Brood of vipers! How can you, being evil, speak good things? For out of the abundance of the heart the mouth speaks. A good man out of the good treasure of his heart brings forth good things, and an evil man out of the evil treasure brings forth evil things. But I say to you, that for every idle word men may speak, they will give account of it in the day of judgment. For by your words you will be justified, and by your words you will be condemned."

The Scribes and Pharisees Ask for a Sign

While the crowds were packed closely together, some of the scribes and Pharisees answered, saying, "Teacher, we want to see a sign from You."

But Jesus answered and said, "This is an evil generation. An evil and adulterous generation who seek after a sign, and no sign will be given to them except the sign of the prophet Jonah. For as Jonah was three days and three nights in the belly of the great fish, so will the Son of Man be three days and three nights in the heart of the earth. The queen of the South will rise up in the judgment with the men of this generation and condemn it, because they repented at the preaching of Jonah; for she came from the ends of the earth to hear the wisdom of Solomon; and indeed, a greater than Solomon is here.

An Unclean Spirit Returns

"When an unclean spirit goes out of a man, he goes through dry places, seeking rest, and finds none. Then he says, 'I will return to my house from which I came.' And when he comes, he finds it empty, swept, and put in order. Then he goes and takes with him seven other spirits more wicked than himself, and they enter and live there; and the last state of that man is worse than the first. It will also be the same with this wicked generation."

Jesus' Mother and Brothers Send for Him

While Jesus was still talking to the multitudes His mother and brothers stood outside, wanting to speak with Him. They could not approach Him because of the crowd, so they sent to Him, asking Him to come out. And many were sitting around Him; and they said to Him, "Look, Your mother and Your brothers are outside asking for You." And again, one said to Him, "Your mother and Your brothers are standing outside, wanting to speak with You."

But Jesus answered and said to the one who told Him, "Who is My mother and who are My brothers?" And He stretched out His hand toward His disciples and said, "Here are My mother and My brothers! For whoever does the will of My Father in heaven, whoever does the will of God, is My brother and sister and mother."

Keeping the Word

And it happened, as Jesus spoke these things, that a certain woman from the crowd raised her voice and said to Him, "Blessed is the womb that bore You, and the breasts which nursed You!"

But He said, "More than that, blessed are those who hear the word of God and keep it!"

The Lamp of the Body

And Jesus continued teaching, saying "No one, when he has lit a lamp, puts it in a secret place or under a basket, but on a lampstand, that those who come in may see the light. The lamp of the body is the eye. Therefore, when your eye is good, your whole body also is full of light. But when your eye is bad, your body also is full of darkness. Take care that the light which is in you is not darkness. If then your whole body is full of light, having no part dark, the whole body will be full of light, as when the bright shining of a lamp gives you light."

Matthew 13:1-52, Mark 4:1-34, Luke 8:1-18, Luke 13:18-21

The Parable of the Sower

On the same day Jesus went out of the house and sat by the sea. And great multitudes were gathered together to Him from every city, so that He got into a boat and sat in it on the sea, and the whole multitude stood on the shore facing the sea.

Then He spoke and taught many things to them in parables saying, "Listen! Behold, a sower went out to sow. And it happened, as he sowed, some seed fell by the wayside; and it was trampled down, and the birds of the air came and devoured them. Some fell on stony ground, rocks or places, where they did not have much earth; and they immediately sprang up because they had no depth of earth. But when the sun was up they were scorched, and because they had no root they withered away, lacking moisture. And some fell among thorns, and the thorns sprang up and choked them and it yielded no crop. But other seed fell on good ground and yielded a crop that sprang up, increased and produced, some a hundredfold, some sixty, some thirty."

When He said these things He cried, "He who has ears to hear, let him hear!"

The Purpose of Parables

But when Jesus was alone, those around Him with the twelve asked Him about the parable. And the disciples came and said to Him, "Why do You speak to them in parables?"

He answered and said to them, "Because it has been given to you to know the mysteries of the kingdom of heaven, but to those who are outside, it has not been given. For whoever has, to him more will be given, and he will have an abundance; but whoever does not have, even what he has will be taken away from him. So, I speak to them in parables, because seeing they do not see, and hearing they do not hear, nor do they understand; in case they should turn, and their sins be forgiven them. And in them the prophecy of Isaiah is fulfilled, which says:

'Hearing you will hear and shall not understand,
And seeing you will see and not perceive;
For the hearts of this people have grown dull'.
Their ears are hard of hearing,
And their eyes they have closed,
In case they should see with their eyes and hear with their ears,
In case they should understand with their hearts and turn,
So that I should heal them.

"But blessed are your eyes for they see, and your ears for they hear. I say to you that many prophets and righteous men desired to see what you see, and did not see it, and to hear what you hear, and did not hear it."

The Parable of the Sower Explained

And Jesus said to them, "Do you not understand this parable? How then will you understand all the parables? The sower sows the word. When anyone hears the word of the kingdom, and does not understand it, then the wicked one, Satan, comes and snatches away the word that was sown in his heart in case they should believe and be saved.

This is he who received the seed by the wayside. These are the ones sown on stony ground or rock, when they hear the word, immediately receive it with gladness, with joy; but they have no root in themselves, and so endure only for a time. Afterward, when tribulation or persecution come for the word's sake, immediately they stumble. Now these are the ones sown among thorns; they are those who hear the word, and the cares of this world, the deceitfulness of riches, and the pleasures of life, desires for other things, enter in and choke the word, and he becomes unfruitful, and bring no fruit to maturity. But he who received the seed sown on the good ground, is he who hears the word with a pure and good heart, and understands it, accepts it, keep it, and bears fruit and produces some a hundredfold, some sixty, some thirty with patience."

The Parable of the Wheat and the Tares

Another parable Jesus shared with them, saying: "The kingdom of heaven is like a man who sowed good seed in his field; but while the men slept, his enemy came and sowed tares among the wheat and went his way. But when the grain had sprouted and produced a crop, then the tares also appeared. The servants of the owner came and said to him, 'Sir, did you not sow good seed in your field? How then does it have tares?' He said to them, 'An enemy has done this.' The servants said to him, 'Do you want us then to go and gather them up?' But he said, 'No, in case while you gather up the tares you also uproot the wheat with them. Let both grow together until the harvest, and at the time of harvest I will say to the reapers, "First gather together the tares and bind them in bundles to burn them, but gather the wheat into my barn.""

The Parable of the Mustard Seed

Jesus shared another parable with them, saying, "To what shall we liken the kingdom of God? Or with what parable shall we picture it? The kingdom of heaven is like a mustard seed, which a man took and sowed in his field, which is the least, smaller than all the seeds on the earth; but when it is sown, it grows up and becomes greater than the herbs and becomes a tree, and shoots out large branches, so that the birds of the air come and nest in its branches, and rest under its shade."

The Parable of the Leaven

And again, Jesus spoke another parable to them. "To what shall I liken the kingdom of God? It is like leaven, which a woman took and hid in three measures of meal till it was all leavened."

Prophecy and the Parables

All these things Jesus spoke to the multitude in parables; and without a parable He did not speak to them, that it might be fulfilled which was spoken by the prophet, saying:

"I will open My mouth in parables;
I will utter things kept secret from
the foundation of the world."

The Parable of the Tares Explained

Then Jesus sent the multitude away and went into the house. And His disciples came to Him, saying, "Explain to us the parable of the tares of the field."

He answered and said to them: "He who sows the good seed is the Son of Man. The field is the world, the good seeds are the sons of the kingdom, but the tares are the sons of the wicked one. The enemy who sowed them is the devil, the harvest is the end of the age, and the reapers are the angels. As the tares are gathered and burned in the fire, so it will be at the end of this age. The Son of Man will send out His angels, and they will gather out of His kingdom all things that offend, and those who practice lawlessness, and will throw them into the furnace of fire. There will be wailing and gnashing of teeth. Then the righteous will shine bright as the sun in the kingdom of their Father. He who has ears to hear, let him hear!

The Parable of the Hidden Treasure

"Again, the kingdom of heaven is like treasure hidden in a field, which a man found and hid; and for joy over it, he goes and sells all that he has and buys that field.

The Parable of the Pearl of Great Price

"Again, the kingdom of heaven is like a merchant seeking beautiful pearls, who, when he had found one pearl of great price, went and sold all that he had and bought it.

The Parable of the Dragnet

"Again, the kingdom of heaven is like a dragnet that was cast into the sea and gathered some of every kind of fish, which, when it was full, the fishermen pulled to shore; and they sat down and gathered the good into containers, but threw the bad away. So, it will be at the end of the age. The angels will come and separate the wicked from among the just, and cast them into the furnace of fire. There will be wailing and gnashing of teeth." Jesus said to them, "Have you understood all these things?"

They said to Him, "Yes, Lord."

Then He said to them, "Every scribe instructed concerning the kingdom of heaven is like a householder who brings out of his treasured things new and old."

The Parable of the Revealed Light or Light Under a Basket

Jesus said to them, "Is a lamp purchased to be put under a basket or under a bed? Is it not to be set on a lampstand?

No one, when he has lit a lamp, covers it with a cloth or puts it under a bed, but sets it on a lampstand, that those who enter may see the light. For there is nothing hidden, which will not be revealed, nor has anything been kept secret but that it should come to light. If anyone has ears to hear, let him hear."

Then He said to them, "Take note what you hear. With the same measure you use, it will be measured to you; and to you who hear, more will be given. For whoever has, to him more will be given; but whoever does not have, even what he seems to have will be taken away from him."

The Parable of the Growing Seed

And Jesus said, "The kingdom of God is like a man who would scatter seed on the ground, and should sleep by night and rise by day. The seed would sprout and grow, but he doesn't know how.

For the earth yields crops by itself: first the blade, then the head, after that the full grain in the head. But when the grain ripens, immediately he puts in the sickle, because the harvest has come."

Jesus' Use of Parables

And with many such parables Jesus spoke the word to them as they were able to hear it. But without a parable He did not speak to them. And when they were alone, He explained all things to His disciples.

Many Women Minister to Jesus

Now it happened, afterward, Jesus went through every city and village, preaching and bringing the glad tidings of the kingdom of God. And the twelve were with Him, and certain women who had been healed of evil spirits and infirmities. Mary called Magdalene, out of whom had come seven demons, and Joanna the wife of Chuza, Herod's steward, and Susanna, and many others who provided for Him from their substance.

Matthew 8:23-34, Mark 4:35 to 5:20, Luke 8:22-39

Wind and Wave Obey Jesus

On a certain day, when evening had come, Jesus got into a boat and His disciples followed Him. He said to them, "Let us cross over to the other side of the lake." And they launched out. But as they sailed He fell asleep.

Now when they had left the multitude, they took Jesus along in the boat as He was. And other little boats were also with them.

And suddenly a tempest, a great windstorm arose on the sea, and the waves beat into the boat, so that the boat was covered with the waves. The boat was filling with water, and they were in great danger. But Jesus was in the stern, asleep on a pillow. And they came to Him and awoke Him, saying, "Master, Teacher, do you not care that we are perishing? Lord, save us!"

But He said to them, "Why are you fearful, how is it that you have no faith?"

Then He got up from where He was sleeping, and rebuked the wind, and said to the sea, "Peace, be still!" And the wind ceased and there was a great calm.

And they were afraid, and marvelled, saying to one another, "Who can this be? For He commands even the winds and water, and they obey Him!"

A Demon-Possessed Man Healed

Then Jesus and His disciples, came to the other side of the sea, to the country of the Gadarenes, which is opposite Galilee. And when Jesus came out of the boat and stepped onto land, immediately there met Him out of the tombs two men, exceedingly fierce, so that no one could pass that way. They were from the city and had demons for a long time, an unclean spirit, who had their dwelling among the tombs; and no one could bind them, not even with chains, because they had often been bound with shackles and chained. And the chains had been pulled apart by them, and the shackles broken in pieces; neither could anyone tame them. And always, night and day, they were in the mountains, not in a house but in the tombs, wearing no clothes, crying out and cutting themselves with stones.

When they saw Jesus in the distance, one ran, fell down before Him and worshiped Him. He cried out with a loud voice and said,

"What have I to do with You, Jesus, Son of the Most High God? I beg You, I implore You by God that You do not torment me!"

Jesus then commanded the evil spirit, saying, "Come out of this man, unclean spirit!"

Then Jesus asked him, "What is your name?"

And he answered, saying, "My name is Legion; for we are many."

They, the demons, begged Jesus earnestly that He would not send them out of the country, that He would not command them to go out into the abyss.

Now a large herd of swine was feeding there near the mountains. All the demons begged Jesus, saying, "Send us to the swine, that we may enter them."

And at once Jesus gave them permission. Then the unclean spirits went out and entered the swine (there were about two thousand); and the herd ran violently down the steep place into the sea, and drowned in the sea.

When those who fed them saw what had happened, they fled and told it in the city and in the country. And the people went out to see what it was that had happened. Then they came to Jesus, and saw the one who had been demon-possessed and had the legion, sitting and clothed and in his right mind at the feet of Jesus. And they were afraid. And those who saw it told them how it happened to him, by what means he, who had been demon-possessed was healed and about the swine. Then the whole multitude of the surrounding region of the Gadarenes began to plead with Him to depart from their region, for they were seized with great fear.

When Jesus and His disciples got into the boat, he who had been demon-possessed begged Jesus that he might go with Him. However, Jesus did not permit him, but said to him, "Go home to your friends, and tell them what great things the Lord has done for you, and how He has had compassion on you."

And he departed and began to proclaim in Decapolis all that Jesus had done for him; and all marvelled.

Matthew 9:18-34, Mark 5:21-43, Luke 8:40-56

A Girl Restored to Life and a Woman Healed

Now when Jesus had crossed over again by boat to the other side, a great multitude gathered to welcome Him; and He was by the sea. One of the rulers of the synagogue came, whose name was Jairus. And when he saw Jesus, he fell at His feet and begged Him earnestly, saying, "My little daughter lies at the point of death. Come and lay Your hands on her, that she may be healed, and she will live."

So, Jesus went with him, and a great multitude followed Him and walked closely with Him.

Now a certain woman had a flow of blood for twelve years, and had suffered many things from many physicians. She had spent all her livelihood on physicians and could not be healed by any and was no better, but rather grew worse. When she heard about Jesus, she came behind Him in the crowd and touched His garment. For she said, "If only I may touch His clothes, I shall be made well." Immediately the fountain of her blood was dried up, and she felt in her body that she was healed of the affliction.

And Jesus, immediately knowing in Himself that power had gone out of Him, turned around in the crowd and said, "Who touched My clothes?"

When all denied it, Peter and those with him said, "You see the multitude thronging You, and You say, 'Who touched Me?'"

But Jesus said, "Somebody touched Me, for I perceived power going out from Me." And He looked around to see who had done this thing.

Now when the woman saw that she was not hidden came fearing and trembling, knowing what had happened to her, came and fell down before Jesus and told Him the whole truth.

He said to her, "Daughter, be of good cheer. Your faith has made you well. Go in peace, and be healed of your affliction."

And the woman was made well from that hour.

While He was still speaking, some came from the ruler of the synagogue's house who said, "Your daughter is dead. Why trouble the Teacher any further?"

As soon as Jesus heard the word that was spoken, He said to the ruler of the synagogue, "Do not be afraid; only believe, and she will be made well." And He permitted no one to follow Him except Peter, James, and John the brother of James.

Then He came to the house of the ruler of the synagogue, and saw the flute players and those who wept and wailed loudly. When He came in, He said to them, "Why make this commotion and weep? The child is not dead, but sleeping."

And they ridiculed Him, knowing that she was dead.

But when He had put the crowd outside, He took the father and the mother of the child, and those who were with Him, and entered where the child was lying. Then He took the child by the hand, and said to her, "Talitha, cumi," which is translated, "Little girl, I say to you, get up!"

Immediately the girl woke and walked, for she was twelve years of age. And they were astonished, and overcome with great amazement. But He commanded them strictly that no one should know it, and that she should be given something to eat. And the report of this went out into all that land.

Two Blind Men Healed

When Jesus departed from there, two blind men followed Him, crying out and saying, "Son of David, have mercy on us!"

And when He had come into the house, the blind men came to Him. And Jesus said to them, "Do you believe that I am able to do this?"

They said to Him, "Yes, Lord."

Then He touched their eyes, saying, "According to your faith let it be to you."

And their eyes were opened. And Jesus sternly warned them, saying, "See that no one knows it."

But when they had departed, they spread the news about Him in all that country.

A Mute Man Speaks

As Jesus and His disciples went out, they brought to Him a man, mute and demon-possessed. And when the demon was cast out, the mute spoke. And the multitudes marvelled, saying, "It was never seen like this in Israel!"

But the Pharisees said, "He casts out demons by the ruler of the demons."

Matthew 13:53-58, Mark 6:1-6

Jesus Rejected at Nazareth

Now, when Jesus had finished these parables, He departed from there, and His disciples followed Him. When He came to His own country, He taught them in their synagogue, when the Sabbath had come. And many hearing Him were astonished, saying, "Where did this Man get this wisdom and these mighty works? What wisdom is this which is given to Him, that such mighty works are performed by His hands! Is this not the carpenter, the Son of Mary, and brother of James, Joses, Judas, and Simon? And are not His sisters here with us?" So, they were offended at Him.

But Jesus said to them, "A prophet is not without honour except in his own country, among his own relatives, and in his own house."

Now He could do no mighty work there, except that He laid His hands on a few sick people and healed them. And He marvelled because of their unbelief. Then He went about the villages in a circuit, teaching.

John 5:1-47

A Man Healed at the Pool of Bethesda

After this there was a feast of the Jews, and Jesus went up to Jerusalem. Now there is in Jerusalem by the Sheep Gate a pool, which is called in Hebrew, Bethesda, having five porches. In these lay a great multitude of sick people, blind, lame, paralyzed, waiting for the moving of the water. For an angel went down at a certain time into the pool and stirred up the water; then whoever stepped in first, after the stirring of the water, was made well of whatever disease he had.

Now a certain man was there who had an infirmity thirty-eight years. When Jesus saw him lying there, and knew that he already had been in that condition a long time, He said to him, "Do you want to be made well?"

The sick man answered Him, "Sir, I have no man to put me into the pool when the water is stirred up; but while I am coming, another steps down before me."

Jesus said to him, "Stand! Take up your bed and walk."

And immediately the man was made well, took up his bed, and walked. And that day was the Sabbath.

For this reason, the Jews said to him who was cured, "It is the Sabbath; it is not lawful for you to carry your bed."

He answered them, "He who made me well said to me, 'Take up your bed and walk.'"

Then they asked him, "Who is the Man who said to you, 'Take up your bed and walk'?" But the one who was healed did not know who it was, for Jesus had left, and there were many people in that place.

A little later, Jesus found him in the temple, and said to him, "See, you have been made well. Sin no more, unless a worse thing come upon you."

The man departed and told the Jews that it was Jesus who had made him well.

Honour the Father and the Son

This was the reason, the Jews persecuted Jesus, and sought to kill Him, because He had done these things on the Sabbath. But Jesus answered them, "My Father has been working until now, and I have been working."

So, the Jews sought all the more to kill Him, because He not only broke the Sabbath, but also said that God was His Father, making Himself equal with God.

Then Jesus said to them, "I say to you, the Son can do nothing of Himself, but what He sees the Father do; for whatever He does, the Son also does in like manner. For the Father loves the Son, and shows Him all things that He Himself does; and He will show Him greater works than these, that you may marvel. For as the Father raises the dead and gives life to them, even so the Son gives life to whom He will. For the Father judges no one, but has committed all judgment to the Son, that all should honour the Son just as they honour the Father. He who does not honour the Son does not honour the Father who sent Him.

Life and Judgment Are Through the Son

"I say to you, he who hears My word and believes in Him who sent Me has everlasting life, and shall not come into judgment, but has passed from death into life. I say to you, the hour is coming, and now is, when the dead will hear the voice of the Son of God; and those who hear will live. For as the Father has life in Himself, so He has granted the Son to have life in Himself, and has given Him authority to execute judgment also, because He is the Son of Man. Do not marvel at this; for the hour is coming in which all who are in the graves will hear His voice and come forth, those who have done good, to the resurrection of life, and those who have done evil, to the resurrection of condemnation. I can of Myself do nothing. As I hear, I judge; and My judgment is righteous, because I do not seek My own will but the will of the Father who sent Me.

The Fourfold Witness

"If I bear witness of Myself, My witness is not true. There is another who bears witness of Me, and I know that the witness which He witnesses of Me is true. You have sent to John, and he has borne witness to the truth. Yet I do not receive testimony from man, but I say these things that you may be saved. He was the burning and shining lamp, and you were willing for a time to rejoice in his light. But I have a greater witness than John's; for the works which the Father has given Me to finish, the very works that I do, bear witness of Me, that the Father has sent Me. And the Father Himself, who sent Me, has testified of Me. You have neither heard His voice at any time, nor seen His form. But you do not have His word abiding in you, because whom He sent, Him you do not believe. You search the Scriptures, for in them you think you have eternal life; and these are they which testify of Me. But you are not willing to come to Me that you may have life. I do not receive honour from men. But I know you, that you do not have the love of God in you. I have come in My Father's name, and you do not receive Me; if another comes in his own name, him you will receive. How can you believe, who receive honour from one another, and do not seek the honour that comes from the only God? Do not think that I shall accuse you to the Father; there is one who accuses you, Moses, in whom you trust. For if you believed Moses, you would believe Me; for he wrote about Me. But if you do not believe his writings, how will you believe My words?"

Matthew 9:35 to 11:1, Mark 6:7-13, Luke 9:1-6

The Compassion of Jesus

Then Jesus went about all the cities and villages, teaching in their synagogues, preaching the gospel of the kingdom, and healing every sickness and every disease among the people. But when He saw the multitudes, He was moved with compassion for them, because they were weary and scattered, like sheep having no shepherd. Then He said to His disciples, "The harvest truly is plentiful, but the labourers are few. Pray the Lord of the harvest to send out labourers into His harvest."

The Twelve Apostles

And when Jesus had called His twelve disciples, He gave them power over unclean spirits, to cast them out, and to heal all kinds of sickness and all kinds of disease. Now the names of the twelve apostles are these: first, Simon, who is called Peter, and Andrew his brother; James the son of Zebedee, and John his brother; Philip and Bartholomew; Thomas and Matthew the tax collector; James the son of Alphaeus, and Lebbaeus, whose surname was Thaddaeus; Simon the Cananite, and Judas Iscariot, who also betrayed Him.

Sending Out the Twelve

These twelve Jesus sent out. He called His twelve disciples together and gave them power and authority over all demons, and to cure diseases. He sent them to preach the kingdom of God and to heal the sick. Jesus commanded them, saying: "Do not go into the way of the Gentiles, and do not enter a city of the Samaritans. But go rather to the lost sheep of the house of Israel. And as you go, preach, saying, 'The kingdom of heaven is at hand.' Heal the sick, cleanse the lepers, raise the dead, cast out demons. Freely you have received, freely give. Provide neither gold nor silver nor copper in your money belts, nor bag for your journey, nor two tunics, nor sandals, nor staffs; for a worker is worthy of his food.

"Now whatever city or town you enter, inquire who in it is worthy, and stay there till you go out. And when you go into a household, greet it. If the household is worthy, let your peace come upon it. But if it is not worthy, let your peace return to you. And whoever will not receive you or hear your words, when you depart from that house or city, shake off the dust from your feet. I say to you, it will be more tolerable for the land of Sodom and Gomorrah in the day of judgment than for that city!"

Persecutions Are Coming

Jesus also told them, "I send you out as sheep in the midst of wolves. Be wise as serpents and harmless as doves. But beware of men, for they will deliver you up to councils and torture you in their synagogues. You will be brought before governors and kings for My sake, as a testimony to them and to the Gentiles. But when they deliver you up, do not worry about how or what you should speak. For it will be given to you in that hour what you should speak; for it is not you who speak, but the Spirit of your Father who speaks in you.

"Now brother will deliver up brother to death, and a father his child; and children will rise up against parents and cause them to be put to death. And you will be hated by all for My name's sake. But he who endures to the end will be saved. When they persecute you in this city, flee to another. I say to you, you will not have gone through the cities of Israel before the Son of Man comes.

"A disciple is not above his teacher, nor a servant above his master. It is enough for a disciple that he be like his teacher, and a servant like his master. If they have called the master of the house Beelzebub, how much more will they call those of his household! Do not fear them. For there is nothing covered that will not be revealed, and hidden that will not be known.

Jesus Teaches the Fear of God

"Whatever I tell you in the dark, speak in the light; and what you hear in the ear, preach on the housetops. And do not fear those who kill the body but cannot kill the soul. But rather fear Him who is able to destroy both soul and body in hell. Are not two sparrows sold for a copper coin? And not one of them falls to the ground apart from your Father's will. But the very hairs of your head are all numbered. Do not fear, because you are of more value than many sparrows.

Confess Christ Before Men

"I tell you the truth, whoever confesses Me before men, him I will also confess before My Father who is in heaven. But whoever denies Me before men, him I will also deny before My Father who is in heaven.

Christ Brings Division

"Do not think that I came to bring peace on earth. I did not come to bring peace but a sword. For I have come to *'set a man against his father, a daughter against her mother, and a daughter-in-law against her mother-in-law'*; and *'a man's enemies will be those of his own household.'* He who loves his father or mother more than Me is not worthy of Me. And he who loves a son or daughter more than Me is not worthy of Me. And he who does not take his cross and follow after Me is not worthy of Me. He who finds his life will lose it, and he who loses his life for My sake will find it.

A Cup of Cold Water

"He who receives you receives Me. He who receives Me receives Him who sent Me. He who receives a prophet in the name of a prophet shall receive a prophet's reward. And he who receives a righteous man in the name of a righteous man shall receive a righteous man's reward. And whoever gives one of these little ones only a cup of cold water in the name of a disciple, I say to you, he shall by no means lose his reward."

Jesus Sends Out the Twelve

When Jesus finished teaching and sharing with His twelve disciples, they departed from there to teach and to preach in their cities, and went through the towns, preaching the gospel and healing everywhere. And they cast out many demons, and anointed with oil many who were sick, and healed them. They went out two by two and preached that people should repent.

Matthew 14:1-12, Mark 6:14-29

John the Baptist Beheaded

At that time Herod, the tetrarch, laid hold of John and bound him, and put him in prison for the sake of Herodias, his brother Philip's wife, because John had said to him, "It is not lawful for you to have your brother's wife."

Herodias held it against John and wanted to kill him, but she could not; for Herod feared John, and the multitude, because they counted him as a prophet. Herod, knew that John was a just and holy man, and protected him. And when Herod had listened and saw the many things he did, he gladly received them.

Then an opportune day came when Herod, on his birthday, gave a feast for his nobles, the high officers, and the chief men of Galilee. During the celebration, Herodias' daughter herself came in and danced, and pleased Herod and those who sat with him, the king said to the girl, "Ask me whatever you want, and I will give it to you." He also promised her, "Whatever you ask me, I will give you, up to half my kingdom."

So, she went out and said to her mother, "What shall I ask?"

And Herodias said, "The head of John the Baptist!"

Immediately she came in with haste to the king and asked, saying, "I want you to give me at once the head of John the Baptist on a platter."

And the king was exceedingly sorry; yet, because of the promises and because of those who sat with him, he did not want to refuse her. Immediately the king sent an executioner and commanded his head to be brought. And he went and beheaded him in prison, brought his head on a platter, and gave it to the girl; and the girl gave it to her mother. When his disciples heard of it, they came and took away his corpse and laid it in a tomb.

Luke 9:7-9

Herod Seeks to See Jesus

Now King Herod heard of Jesus, and all that was done by Him; for His name had become well known. And he said, "John the Baptist is risen from the dead, and for this reason these powers are at work in him." Others said, "It is Elijah." And others said, "It is the Prophet, or like one of the prophets." But when Herod heard, he was perplexed and said, "This is John, whom I beheaded; he has been raised from the dead!" So, he sought to see Jesus.

Matthew 14:13-21, Mark 6:30-44, Luke 9:10-17, John 6:1-15

Feeding the Five Thousand Jews

Then the apostles gathered to Jesus and told Him all things, both what they had done and what they had taught. And He said to them, "Come aside by yourselves to a deserted place and rest a while."

There were many coming and going, and they did not even have time to eat. So, they departed and went over the Sea of Galilee, which is the Sea of Tiberias to a deserted place in the boat by themselves. But the multitudes saw them departing, and many knew Him and ran there on foot from all the cities. And Jesus went up on the mountain, and there He sat with His disciples.

Now the Passover, a feast of the Jews, was near. The people arrived before Jesus and His disciples, and came together to Him because they saw His signs which He performed on those who were diseased. And Jesus, when He came out, saw a great multitude and was moved with compassion for them, because they were like sheep not having a shepherd. So, He began to teach them many things about the kingdom of God, and healed those who had need of healing.

When it was evening, His disciples came to Him, saying, "This is a deserted place, and the hour is already late. Send the multitudes away, that they may go into the surrounding towns and country, and lodge and buy themselves food."

But Jesus said to them, "They do not need to go away. You give them something to eat." He said to Philip, "Where shall we buy bread, that these may eat?" But this Jesus said to test him, for He Himself knew what He would do.

Philip answered Him, "Two hundred denarii worth of bread is not sufficient for them, that every one of them may have a little."

One of His disciples, Andrew, Simon Peter's brother, said to Him, "There is a lad here who has five barley loaves and two small fish, but what are they among so many?"

Then Jesus said, "Bring them here to Me." Then He commanded the multitudes to sit down on the grass.

Now there was much grass in the place. So, the men sat down, in number about five thousand. And Jesus took the loaves, and when He had given thanks He distributed them to the disciples, and the disciples to those sitting down; and likewise of the fish, as much as they wanted.

So, when they were filled, He said to His disciples, "Gather up the fragments that remain, so that nothing is lost."

Therefore, they gathered them up, and filled twelve baskets with the fragments of the five barley loaves which were left over by those who had eaten. Then those men, when they had seen the sign that Jesus did, said, "This is truly the Prophet who is to come into the world."

Jesus perceived that they were about to come and take Him by force to make Him king.

Matthew 14:22-33, Mark 6:45-52, John 6:16-21

Jesus Walks on the Sea

Then Jesus made His disciples get into the boat and go before Him to the other side, toward Capernaum while He sent the multitudes away. And when He had sent the multitudes away, He went up alone on the mountain by Himself to pray.

Now when evening came, He was alone there. But the boat was now in the middle of the sea, tossed by the waves. Then Jesus saw His disciples straining at rowing, for the wind was against them.

Now about the fourth watch of the night He came to them, walking on the sea, and He would have passed them by. They had rowed about three or four miles, when the disciples saw Jesus walking on the sea and drawing near the boat; and they were afraid. For when they saw Him walking on the sea, they supposed it was a ghost, and cried out; for they all saw Him and were troubled.

But immediately He talked with them and said to them, "Be of good cheer! It is I; do not be afraid."

And Peter answered Him and said, "Lord, if it is You, command me to come to You on the water."

Jesus replied, "Come."

And when Peter had climbed down out of the boat, he walked on the water to go to Jesus. But when he saw that the wind was boisterous, he was afraid; and beginning to sink he cried out, saying, "Lord, save me!"

And without hesitation, Jesus stretched out His hand and caught him, and said to him, "O you of little faith, why did you doubt?"

Then they went up into the boat to the other disciples, and the wind ceased. Those who were in the boat came and worshiped Him, saying, "Truly You are the Son of God." And they were greatly amazed in themselves beyond measure, and marvelled, for they had not understood about the loaves, because their heart was hardened. And at once, the boat was at the land where they were going.

Matthew 14:34-36, Mark 6:53-56

Many Touch Him and Are Made Well

When Jesus and His disciples had crossed over, they came to the land of Gennesaret and anchored there. And when they came out of the boat, immediately the people of that place recognized Him. This news spread quickly through that whole surrounding region.

The people carried many who were sick, on beds to wherever they heard He was. Whenever He entered into villages, cities, or the country, they laid the sick in the marketplaces, and begged Him that they might just touch the hem of His garment. And as many as touched Him were made well.

John 6:22-71

The Bread from Heaven

On the following day, the people who were standing on the other side of the sea saw that there was no other boat there, except the one which His disciples had entered, and that Jesus had not entered the boat with His disciples, but His disciples had gone away alone. Other boats came from Tiberias, near the place where they ate bread after the Lord had given thanks. When the people saw that Jesus was not there, nor His disciples, they also got into boats and came to Capernaum, seeking Jesus. And when they found Him on the other side of the sea, they said to Him, "Rabbi, how and when did You come here?"

Jesus answered them and said, "I say to you, you looked for Me, not because you saw the signs, but because you ate of the loaves and were filled. Do not labour for the food which perishes, but for the food which endures to everlasting life, which the Son of Man will give you, because God the Father has set His seal on Him."

Then they said to Him, "What shall we do, that we may work the works of God?"

Jesus answered and said to them, "This is the work of God, that you believe in Him whom He sent."

Therefore, they said to Him, "What sign will You perform then, that we may see it and believe You? What work will You do? Our fathers ate the manna in the desert; as it is written, *'He gave them bread from heaven to eat.'"*

Then Jesus said to them, "I say to you, Moses did not give you the bread from heaven, but My Father gives you the true bread from heaven. For the bread of God is He who comes down from heaven and gives life to the world."

Then they said to Him, "Lord, give us this bread always."

And Jesus said to them, "I am the bread of life. He who comes to Me shall never hunger, and he who believes in Me shall never thirst. But I said to you that you have seen Me and yet you do not believe. All that the Father gives Me will come to Me, and the one who comes to Me I will by no means cast out. For I have come down from heaven, not to do My own will, but the will of Him who sent Me. This is the will of the Father who sent Me, that of all He has given Me I should lose nothing, but should raise it up at the last day. And this is the will of Him who sent Me, that everyone who sees the Son and believes in Him may have everlasting life; and I will raise him up at the last day."

Rejected by His Own

The Jews then complained about Jesus, because He said, "I am the bread which came down from heaven." And they said, "Is not this Jesus, the son of Joseph, whose father and mother we know? How is it then that He says, 'I have come down from heaven'?"

Jesus answered and said to them, "Do not murmur among yourselves. No one can come to Me unless the Father who sent Me draws him; and I will raise him up at the last day. It is written in the prophets, *'And they shall all be taught by God.'* For this reason, everyone who has heard and learned from the Father comes to Me. Not that anyone has seen the Father, except He who is from God; He has seen the Father. I say to you, he who believes in Me has everlasting life. I am the bread of life. Your fathers ate the manna in the wilderness, and are dead. This is the bread which comes down from heaven, that one may eat of it and not die. I am the living bread which came down from heaven. If anyone eats of this bread, he will live forever; and the bread that I shall give is My flesh, which I shall give for the life of the world."

The Jews therefore quarrelled among themselves, saying, "How can this Man give us His flesh to eat?"

Then Jesus said to them, "I say to you, unless you eat the flesh of the Son of Man and drink His blood, you have no life in you. Whoever eats My flesh and drinks My blood has eternal life, and I will raise him up at the last day. For My flesh is food, and My blood is drink. He who eats My flesh and drinks My blood, abides in Me, and I in him. As the living Father sent Me, and I live because of the Father, so he who feeds on Me will live because of Me. This is the bread which came down from heaven, not as your fathers ate the manna, and are dead. He who eats this bread will live forever."

These things He said in the synagogue as He taught in Capernaum.

Many Disciples Turn Away

Many of Jesus' disciples, when they heard this, said, "This is a hard saying; who can understand it?"

When Jesus knew in Himself that His disciples complained about this, He said to them, "Does this offend you? What then if you should see the Son of Man ascend where He was before? It is the Spirit who gives life; the flesh profits nothing. The words that

I speak to you are spirit, and they are life. But there are some of you who do not believe." For Jesus knew from the beginning who they were who did not believe, and who would betray Him. And He said, "Therefore I have said to you that no one can come to Me unless it has been granted to him by My Father."

From that time, many of His disciples went back and walked with Him no more. Then Jesus said to the twelve, "Do you also want to go away?"

But Simon Peter answered Him, "Lord, to whom shall we go? You have the words of eternal life. Also, we have come to believe and know that You are the Christ, the Son of the living God."

Jesus answered them, "Did I not choose you, the twelve, and one of you is a devil?"

He spoke of Judas Iscariot, the son of Simon, for it was he who would betray Him, being one of the twelve.

Matthew 15:1-20, Mark 7:1-23

Defilement Comes from Within

Then the Pharisees and some of the scribes from Jerusalem came to Jesus. Now when they saw some of His disciples eat bread with defiled, that is, with unwashed hands, they found fault. For the Pharisees and all the Jews do not eat unless they wash their hands in a special way, holding the tradition of the elders. When they come from the marketplace, they do not eat unless they wash. And there are many other things which they have received and hold, like the washing of cups, pitchers, copper vessels, and couches.

Then the Pharisees and scribes asked Him, "Why do Your disciples transgress the tradition of the elders, for they do not wash their hands when they eat bread?"

Jesus answered and said to them, "Why do you also transgress the commandment of God because of your tradition? For God commanded, saying, *'Honour your father and your mother'*; and, *'He who curses father or mother, let him be put to death.'* But you say, 'Whoever says to his father or mother, "Whatever profit you might have received from me is a gift to God", then he need not honour his father or mother.' Thus, you have made the commandment of God of no effect by your tradition, which you have handed down. And many such things you do. Hypocrites! Well did Isaiah prophesy about you, saying:

'These people draw near to Me with their mouth,
And honour Me with their lips,
But their heart is far from Me.
And in vain they worship Me,
Teaching as doctrines the commandments of men.'

"Putting aside the commandment of God, you hold the tradition of men, the washing of pitchers and cups, and many other such things you do."

Jesus said to them, "All too well you reject the commandment of God, that you may keep your tradition."

When He had called the multitude to Himself, He said to them, "Hear and understand. There is nothing that goes into the mouth will defile a man; but what comes out of the mouth, this defiles a man. If anyone has ears to hear, let him hear!"

When He had entered a house away from the crowd, Peter, one of His disciples, asked Him to explain the parable to them.

So, He said to them, "Are you still without understanding also? Do you not perceive that whatever enters a man from outside cannot defile him, because it does not enter his heart but his stomach, and is eliminated, purifying all foods?" And He said, "What comes out of a man, that defiles a man, comes from within. Out of the heart of men, proceed evil thoughts, adulteries, fornications, murders, thefts, covetousness, wickedness, deceit, obscenities, an evil eye, blasphemy, pride, foolishness. All these evil things come from within and defile a man."

Then His disciples came and said to Him, "Do You know that the Pharisees were offended when they heard this saying?"

But Jesus answered and said, "Every plant which My Heavenly Father has not planted will be uprooted. Let them alone. They are blind leaders of the blind. And if the blind leads the blind, both will fall into a ditch."

Matthew 15:21-31, Mark 7:24-37

A Gentile Shows Her Faith

Then Jesus went out from the land of the Gennesaret, and departed to the region of Tyre and Sidon. And He entered a house and wanted no one to know He was there, but He could not be hidden.

For a woman of Canaan came from that region whose young daughter had an unclean spirit. When she heard about Jesus, and she came and fell at His feet. The woman was a Greek, a Syro-Phoenician by birth, and she kept asking Him to cast the demon out of her daughter. She cried out to Him, saying, "Have mercy on me, O Lord, Son of David! My daughter is severely demon-possessed."

But He answered her not a word. And His disciples came and urged Him, saying, "Send her away, for she cries out after us."

But Jesus answered and said, "I was not sent except to the lost sheep of the house of Israel."

Then she came and worshiped Him, saying, "Lord, help me!"

But Jesus said to her, "Let the children be filled first, for it is not good to take the children's bread and throw it to the little dogs."

And she said, "Yes, Lord, yet even the little dogs under the table eat the children's crumbs which fall from their masters' table."

Then Jesus answered and said to her, "O woman, great is your faith! For this saying go your way; Let it be to you as you desire. The demon has gone out of your daughter."

And her daughter was healed from that very hour. And when she came to her house, she found the demon gone out, and her daughter lying on the bed.

Jesus Heals Great Multitudes

Jesus departed from there, skirted the Sea of Galilee, and went up on the mountain and sat down there. Then great multitudes came to Him, having with them the lame, blind, mute, maimed, and many others; and they laid them down at Jesus' feet, and He healed them. So, the multitude marvelled when they saw the mute speaking, the maimed made whole, the lame walking, and the blind seeing; and they glorified the God of Israel.

Jesus Heals a Deaf-Mute

Again, departing from the region of Tyre and Sidon, Jesus came through the midst of the region of Decapolis to the Sea of Galilee. Then the local people brought to Him one who was deaf and had an impediment in his speech, and they begged Him to put His hand on him. And Jesus took him aside from the multitude, and put His fingers in his ears, and He spat and touched his tongue. Then, looking up to heaven, He sighed, and said to him, "Ephphatha," that is, "Be opened."

At once his ears were opened, and the impediment of his tongue was loosed, and he spoke plainly. Then Jesus commanded them that they should tell no one; but the more He commanded them, the more widely they proclaimed what had happened. And the people were astonished beyond belief, saying, "He has done all things well. He makes both the deaf to hear and the mute to speak."

Matthew 15:32-39, Mark 8:1-10

Feeding the Four Thousand Gentiles

In those days, the multitude being very great and having nothing to eat, Jesus called His disciples to Himself and said to them, "I have compassion on the multitude, because they have now continued with Me three days and have nothing to eat. And if I send them away hungry to their own houses, they will faint on the way; for some of them have come a long distance."

Then His disciples answered Him, "Where could we get enough bread in the wilderness to fill such a great multitude?"

Jesus said to them, "How many loaves do you have?"

And they answered Him saying, "Seven, and a few little fish."

So, He commanded the multitude to sit down on the ground. And He took the seven loaves and the fish and gave thanks, broke them and gave them to His disciples; and the disciples set them before the multitude. So, they all ate and were filled. Afterwards, the disciples took up seven large baskets full of the fragments that were left. Now those who ate were four thousand men, besides women and children. And Jesus sent the multitude away, and immediately got into the boat with His disciples, and came to the region of Dalmanutha.

Matthew 16:1-12, Mark 8:11-26

The Pharisees and Sadducees Seek a Sign

Then the Pharisees and Sadducees came out and began to dispute and to test Him. They asked that Jesus would show them a sign from heaven. But He sighed deeply in His spirit.

Jesus answered and said to them, "When it is evening you say, 'It will be fair weather, for the sky is red'; and in the morning, 'It will be foul weather today, for the sky is red and threatening.' Hypocrites! You know how to discern the face of the sky, but you cannot discern the signs of the times. A wicked and adulterous generation seeks after a sign, and no sign shall be given to it except the sign of the prophet Jonah."

The Leaven of the Pharisees, Sadducees and Herod

And Jesus left them, and getting into the boat again, departed to the other side. Now when His disciples came to the other side, they had forgotten to take bread, and they did not have more than one loaf with them in the boat. Then Jesus said to them, "Take heed and beware of the leaven of the Pharisees, the Sadducees and Herod."

And they talked among themselves, saying, "It is because we have taken no bread."

But Jesus, being aware of what they were saying, said to them, "O you of little faith, why do you talk among yourselves because you have brought no bread? Do you still not understand? Is your heart still hardened? Having eyes, do you not see? And having ears, do you not hear? Don't you remember when I broke the five loaves for the five thousand and how many baskets you took up?"

They said to Him, "Twelve."

"Also, when I broke the seven for the four thousand, how many large baskets full of fragments did you take up?"

And they said, "Seven."

He said to them, "How is it you do not understand that I did not speak to you concerning bread, but to beware of the leaven of the Pharisees, Sadducees and Herod."

Then they understood that He did not tell them to beware of the leaven of bread, but of the doctrine of the Pharisees and Sadducees and Herod.

A Blind Man Healed at Bethsaida

Then Jesus came to Bethsaida; and they brought a blind man to Him, and begged Him to touch him. So, He took the blind man by the hand and led him out of the town. And when He had put spit on his eyes and put His hands on him, Jesus asked him if he saw anything.

And he looked up and said, "I see men like trees, walking."

Then Jesus put His hands on his eyes again and made him look up. And his eyes were restored and he saw everyone clearly. Then He sent him away to his house, saying, "Don't go into the town, or tell anyone in the town."

Matthew 16:13-28, Mark 8:27 to 9:1, Luke 9:18-27

Peter Confesses Jesus as the Christ

Jesus came into the region of Caesarea Philippi. And it happened, as He was alone praying, that His disciples joined Him. Jesus asked His disciples, "Who do men say that I, the Son of Man, am?"

So they said, "Some say John the Baptist, but some Elijah, and others Jeremiah or one of the prophets has risen again."

He said to them, "But who do you say that I am?"

Simon Peter answered and said, "You are the Christ, the Son of the living God."

Jesus answered and said to him, "Blessed are you, Simon Bar-Jonah, for flesh and blood has not revealed this to you, but My Father who is in heaven. And I also say to you, that you are Peter, and on this rock, I will build My church, and the gates of Hades shall not prevail against it. And I will give you the keys of the kingdom of heaven, and whatever you bind on earth will be bound in heaven, and whatever you loose on earth will be loosed in heaven."

Then He strictly commanded His disciples that they should tell no one that He was Jesus the Christ.

Jesus Predicts His Death and Resurrection

From that time, Jesus began to show and teach His disciples that He must go to Jerusalem, and suffer many things, and be rejected by the elders and chief priests and scribes, and be killed, and after three days rise again. He spoke this word openly.

Then Peter took Him aside and began to rebuke Him, saying, "Never, Lord! This shall not happen to You!"

But Jesus turned around and looked at His disciples. Then He turned to Peter and rebuked him saying, "Get behind Me, Satan! You are an offense, a stumbling block to Me, for you are not mindful of the things of God, but the things of men."

Take Up the Cross and Follow Him

When Jesus had called the people to Himself, with His disciples also, He said to them, "Whoever desires to come after Me, let him deny himself, and take up his cross daily, and follow Me. For whoever desires to save his life will lose it, but whoever loses his life for My sake and the gospel's will save it. For what will it profit a man if he gains the whole world, and is himself destroyed or lost and loses his own soul? Or what will a man give in exchange for his soul? For whoever is ashamed of Me and My words in this adulterous and sinful generation, of him the Son of Man also will be ashamed when He comes in the glory of His Father with the holy angels, and then He will reward each according to his works."

And He said to them, "I say to you that there are some standing here who will not taste death till they see the kingdom of God present with power."

Matthew 17:1-13, Mark 9:2-13, Luke 9:28-36

Jesus Transfigured on the Mount

Now after six to eight days Jesus took Peter, James with John his brother, and led them up on a high mountain by themselves to pray. As Jesus prayed, He was transfigured before them. The appearance of His face was altered, and it shone like the sun, and His robe, His clothes became glistening, as white as the light, shining, exceedingly white, like snow, such as no launderer on earth can whiten them.

And Elijah appeared in glory to them with Moses, and they were talking with Jesus, and spoke of His death which He was about to be accomplished at Jerusalem. But Peter and those with him were heavy with sleep; and when they were fully awake, they saw His glory and the two men who stood with Him.

Then it happened, as they were parting from Him, Peter said to Jesus, "Master, Lord, Rabbi, it is good for us to be here; if you wish, let us make three tabernacles: one for You, one for Moses, and one for Elijah", because he did not know what to say, for they were greatly afraid.

While he was still speaking, a bright cloud came and overshadowed them; and they were fearful as they entered the cloud. And suddenly a voice came out of the cloud, saying, "This is My beloved Son, in whom I am well pleased. Hear Him!" And when the disciples heard it, when they had looked around, they saw no one anymore. They fell on their faces and were greatly afraid.

But Jesus came and touched them and said, "Get up, and do not be afraid."

When their eyes were fully opened, they saw no one, only Jesus.

Now as Jesus, Peter, James and John came down from the mountain, Jesus commanded them that they should tell no one the things they had seen, till the Son of Man had risen from the dead. So, they kept this word to themselves, questioning what the rising from the dead meant.

And His disciples asked Him, saying, "Why then do the scribes say that Elijah must come first?"

Jesus answered and said to them, "Elijah is coming first and will restore all things. But I say to you that Elijah has come already and restored all things, and they did not know him but did to him whatever they wished. And how is it written concerning the Son of Man, that He must suffer many things and be treated with contempt at their hands?"

Then the disciples understood that He spoke to them of John the Baptist.

Matthew 17:14-23, Mark 9:14-32, Luke 9:37-45

A Boy Is Healed

Now it happened on the next day, after Jesus had come down from the mountain, He came near to the disciples and saw a great multitude around them, and scribes disputing with them. Immediately, when they saw Him, all the people were greatly amazed, and running to Him, greeted Him. And He asked the scribes, "What are you discussing with My disciples?"

Suddenly a man from the multitude cried out, and came to Jesus, kneeling down to Him and saying, "Lord, I ask you, look on my son, have mercy on my son, who has a mute spirit. He is my only child, an epileptic and suffers severely; for he often falls into the fire and into the water. When a spirit seizes him, he suddenly cries out; it convulses him and throws him down. He foams at the mouth, gnashes his teeth, and becomes ridged. Then it departs from him with great difficulty, bruising him. So, I brought him to Your disciples to cast it out, but they could not."

Jesus answered him and said, "O faithless generation, how long shall I be with you? How long shall I bear with you? Bring your son to Me."

Then they brought the man's son to Jesus. And when the son saw Jesus, immediately the spirit, the demon, convulsed him, and he fell on the ground, rolling around and foaming at the mouth.

Jesus asked his father, "How long has this been happening to him?"

And he said, "From childhood. And often he has been thrown both into the fire and into the water to destroy him. But if You can do anything, have compassion on us and help us."

Jesus said to him, "If you can believe, all things are possible to him who believes."

Immediately the father of the child cried out and said with tears, "Lord, I believe; help my unbelief!"

When Jesus saw that the people came running together, He rebuked the unclean spirit, saying to it, "Deaf and dumb spirit, I command you, come out of him and enter him no more!"

Then the spirit cried out, convulsed him greatly, and came out of him. And he became as one dead, so that many said, "He is dead."

But Jesus took him by the hand and lifted him up, and gave him back to his father. And the child was cured from that hour. And all the people were amazed at the majesty of God, and everyone marvelled at all the things that Jesus did.

And when Jesus came into the house, His disciples said to Him privately, "Why could we not cast it out?"

Jesus said to them, "Because of your unbelief; for I say to you, if you have faith as a mustard seed, you will say to this mountain, 'Move from here to there,' and it will move; and nothing will be impossible for you. However, this kind does not go out except by prayer and fasting."

Jesus Again Predicts His Death and Resurrection

Then Jesus, along with His disciples, departed from there and passed through Galilee and He did not want anyone to know it.

Now while they were staying in Galilee, He taught His disciples and said to them, "Take notice of what I am about to say to you. The Son of Man is being betrayed into the hands of men, and they will kill Him. And after they kill Him, He will rise on the third day."

But they did not understand this saying as it was hidden from them, so that they did not understand it; and they were extremely sorrowful and afraid to ask Him about this saying.

Matthew 17:24 to 18:9, Mark 9:33-50, Luke 9:46-50

Peter and His Master Pay Their Taxes

When Jesus came near to Capernaum, those who received the temple tax came to Peter and said, "Does your Teacher pay the temple tax?"

He said, "Yes."

And when he had come into the house, Jesus anticipated him, saying, "What do you think, Simon? From whom do the kings of the earth take customs or taxes, from their sons or from strangers?"

Peter said to Him, "From strangers."

Jesus said to him, "Then the sons are free. But, in case we offend them, go to the sea, cast in your line, and take the fish that comes up first. And when you have opened its mouth, you will find a piece of money; take that and give it to them for Me and you."

Who Is the Greatest?

Then Jesus came to Capernaum. And when He was in the house He asked them, "What was it you disputed among yourselves on the road?"

But they kept silent, for on the road they had disputed among themselves who would be the greatest.

And Jesus, knowing the thoughts of their heart, sat down, called the twelve, and said to them, "If anyone desires to be first, he shall be last of all and servant of all."

Then the disciples said to Jesus, "Who then is greatest in the kingdom of heaven?"

Then He took a little child and set him in the midst of them. And when He had taken him in His arms, Jesus said to them,

"Whoever receives one of these little children in My name receives Me; and whoever receives Me, receives not Me but Him who sent Me. I say to you, unless you are converted and become as little children, you will by no means enter the kingdom of heaven. Whoever humbles himself as this little child is the greatest in the kingdom of heaven. Whoever receives one little child like this in My name receives Me. For he who is least among you all will be great.

Jesus Warns of Offenses

"But whoever causes one of these little ones who believe in Me to stumble and sin, it would be better for him if a millstone were hung around his neck, and he were drowned in the depth of the sea. Woe to the world because of offenses! For offenses must come, but woe to that man by whom the offense comes! If your hand causes you to sin, cut it off and cast it from you. It is better for you to enter into life maimed, rather than having two hands, to go to hell, into the fire that shall never be quenched, where

'Their worm does not die
And the fire is not quenched.'

"And if your foot causes you to sin, cut it off and cast it from you. It is better for you to enter life lame, rather than having two feet, to be cast into hell, into the everlasting fire that shall never be quenched, where

'Their worm does not die
And the fire is not quenched.'

"And if your eye causes you to sin, pluck it out and cast it from you. It is better for you to enter the kingdom of God with one eye, rather than having two eyes, to be cast into hell fire, where

*'Their worm does not die
And the fire is not quenched.'*

Tasteless Salt Is Worthless

"For everyone will be seasoned with fire, and every sacrifice will be seasoned with salt. Salt is good, but if the salt loses its flavour, how will you season it? Have salt in yourselves, and have peace with one another."

Jesus Forbids Sectarianism

Now John answered Him, saying, "Teacher, we saw someone who does not follow us casting out demons in Your name, and we forbade him because he does not follow us."

But Jesus said, "Do not forbid him, for no one who works a miracle in My name can soon afterward speak evil of Me. For he who is not against us is on our side. For whoever gives you a cup of water to drink in My name, because you belong to Christ, assuredly, I say to you, he will by no means lose his reward."

John 7:1-52

Jesus' Brothers Disbelieve

After these things Jesus walked in Galilee; for He did not want to walk in Judea, because the Jews sought to kill Him.

Now the Jews' Feast of Tabernacles was at hand. Jesus' brothers said to Him, "Depart from here and go into Judea, that Your disciples may also see the works that You are doing. For no one does anything in secret while he himself seeks to be known openly. If You do these things, show Yourself to the world." For even His brothers did not believe in Him.

Then Jesus said to them, "My time has not yet come, but your time is always ready. The world cannot hate you, but it hates Me because I testify of it that its works are evil. You go up to this feast. I am not yet going up to this feast, for My time has not fully come."

When He had said these things to them, He remained in Galilee.

The Heavenly Scholar

But when Jesus' brothers had gone up, then He also went up to the feast, not openly, but as it were in secret. Then the Jews sought Him at the feast, and said, "Where is He?" And there was much complaining among the people concerning Him. Some said, "He is good"; others said, "No, on the contrary, He deceives the people." No one spoke openly about Him for fear of the Jews.

Now about the middle of the feast Jesus went up into the temple and taught. And the Jews marvelled, saying, "How does this Man know letters, having never studied?"

Jesus answered them and said, "My doctrine is not Mine, but His who sent Me. If anyone wills to do His will, he shall know concerning the doctrine, whether it is from God or whether I speak on My own authority. He who speaks from himself seeks his own glory; but He who seeks the glory of the One who sent Him is true, and no unrighteousness is in Him. Did not Moses give you the law, yet none of you keeps the law? Why do you seek to kill Me?"

The people answered and said, "You have a demon. Who is seeking to kill You?"

Jesus answered and said to them, "I did one work, and you all marvel. Moses therefore gave you circumcision (not that it is from Moses, but from the fathers), and you circumcise a man on the Sabbath. If a man receives circumcision on the Sabbath, so that the law of Moses should not be broken, are you angry with Me because I made a man completely well on the Sabbath? Do not judge according to appearance, but judge with righteous judgment."

Could This Be the Christ?

Now some of the people from Jerusalem said, "Is this not He whom they seek to kill? But look! He speaks boldly, and they say nothing to Him. Do the rulers know that this is truly the Christ? However, we know where this Man is from; but when the Christ comes, no one knows where He is from."

Then Jesus cried out, as He taught in the temple, saying, "You both know Me, and you know where I am from; and I have not come of Myself, but He who sent Me is true, whom you do not know. But I know Him, for I am from Him, and He sent Me."

Now, they sought to take Him; but no one laid a hand on Him, because His hour had not yet come. And many of the people believed in Him, and said, "When the Christ comes, will He do more signs than these which this Man has done?"

Jesus and the Religious Leaders

The Pharisees heard the crowd murmuring these things concerning Him, and the Pharisees and the chief priests sent officers to take Him.

Then Jesus said to them, "I shall be with you a little while longer, and then I go to Him who sent Me. You will seek Me and not find Me, and where I am you cannot come."

Then the Jews said among themselves, "Where does He intend to go that we shall not find Him? Does He intend to go to the Dispersion among the Greeks and teach the Greeks? What is this thing that He said, 'You will seek Me and not find Me, and where I am you cannot come'?"

The Promise of the Holy Spirit

On the last day, that great day of the feast, Jesus stood and cried out, saying, "If anyone thirsts, let him come to Me and drink. He who believes in Me, as the Scripture has said, out of his heart will flow rivers of living water."

But this He spoke concerning the Spirit, whom those believing in Him would receive; for the Holy Spirit was not yet given, because Jesus was not yet glorified.

Who Is He?

Then, many from the crowd, when they heard this saying, said, "Truly this is the Prophet." Others said, "This is the Christ."

But some said, "Will the Christ come out of Galilee? Has not the Scripture said that the Christ comes from the seed of David and from the town of Bethlehem, where David was?" So, there was a division among the people because of Him.

Now some of them wanted to take Him, but no one laid hands on Him.

Rejected by the Authorities

Then the officers came to the chief priests and Pharisees, who said to them, "Why have you not brought Him?"

The officers answered, "No man ever spoke like this Man!"

Then the Pharisees answered them, "Are you also deceived? Have any of the rulers or the Pharisees believed in Him? But this crowd that does not know the law, is accursed."

Nicodemus (he who came to Jesus by night, being one of them) said to them, "Does our law judge a man before it hears him and knows what he is doing?"

They answered and said to him, "Are you also from Galilee? Search and look, for no prophet has originated out of Galilee."

John 7:53 to 8:11

An Adulteress Faces the Light of the World

And everyone went to his own house. But Jesus went to the Mount of Olives.

Now early in the morning He came again into the temple, and all the people came to Him; and He sat down and taught them. Then the scribes and Pharisees brought to Him a woman caught in adultery. And when they had set her in the midst, they said to Him, "Teacher, this woman was caught in adultery, in the very act. Now Moses, in the law, commanded us that such should be stoned. But what do You say?" This they said, testing Him, that they might have something of which to accuse Him.

But Jesus stooped down and wrote on the ground with His finger, as though He did not hear.

So, when they continued asking Him, He raised Himself up and said to them, "He who is without sin among you, let him throw a stone at her first." And again, He stooped down and wrote on the ground.

Then those who heard it, being convicted by their conscience, went out one by one, beginning with the oldest even to the last. And Jesus was left alone, and the woman standing near Him.

When Jesus stood up and looked around, and saw no one but the woman, He said to her, "Woman, where are those who are accusing you? Has no one condemned you?"

She said, "No one, Lord."

And Jesus said to her, "Neither do I condemn you; go and sin no more."

John 8:12-59

Jesus Defends His Self-Witness

Then Jesus spoke to them again, saying, "I am the light of the world. He who follows Me shall not walk in darkness, but have the light of life."

The Pharisees said to Him, "You bear witness of Yourself; Your witness is not true."

Jesus answered and said to them, "Even if I bear witness of Myself, My witness is true, for I know where I came from and where I am going; but you do not know where I came from and where I am going. You judge according to the flesh; I judge no one. And yet if I do judge, My judgment is true; for I am not alone, but I am with the Father who sent Me. It is also written in your law that the testimony of two men is true. I am One who bears witness of Myself, and the Father who sent Me bears witness of Me."

Then they said to Him, "Where is Your Father?"

Jesus answered, "You know neither Me nor My Father. If you had known Me, you would have known My Father also."

These words Jesus spoke in the treasury, as He taught in the temple; and no one laid hands on Him, for His hour had not yet come.

Jesus Predicts His Departure

Then Jesus said to them again, "I am going away, and you will seek Me, and will die in your sin. Where I go you cannot come."

So the Jews said, "Will He kill Himself, because He says, 'Where I go you cannot come'?"

And He said to them, "You are from beneath; I am from above. You are of this world; I am not of this world. For this reason, I said to you that you will die in your sins; for if you do not believe that I am He, you will die in your sins."

Then they said to Him, "Who are You?"

And Jesus said to them, "Just what I have been saying to you from the beginning. I have many things to say and to judge concerning you, but He who sent Me is true; and I speak to the world those things which I heard from Him."

They did not understand that He spoke to them of the Father.

Then Jesus said to them, "When you lift up the Son of Man, then you will know that I am He, and that I do nothing of Myself; but as My Father taught Me, I speak these things. And He who sent Me is with Me. The Father has not left Me alone, for I always do those things that please Him."

As He spoke these words, many believed in Him.

The Truth Shall Make You Free

Then Jesus said to those Jews who believed Him, "If you believe in My word, you are truly My disciples. And you shall know the truth, and the truth shall make you free."

They answered Him, "We are Abraham's descendants, and have never been in bondage to anyone. How can You say, 'You will be made free'?"

Jesus answered them, "I say to you, whoever commits sin is a slave of sin. And a slave does not abide in the house forever, but a son abides forever. Therefore, if the Son makes you free, you shall be free indeed.

Abraham's Seed and Satan's

"I know that you are Abraham's descendants, but you seek to kill Me, because My word has no place in you. I speak what I have seen with My Father, and you do what you have seen with your father."

They answered and said to Him, "Abraham is our father."

Jesus said to them, "If you were Abraham's children, you would do the works of Abraham. But now you seek to kill Me, a Man who has told you the truth which I heard from God. Abraham did not do this. You do the deeds of your father."

Then they said to Him, "We were not born of fornication; we have one Father, God."

Jesus said to them, "If God were your Father, you would love Me, for I proceeded forth and came from God; nor have I come of Myself, but He sent Me. Why do you not understand My speech? Because you are not able to listen to My word. You are of your father the devil, and the desires of your father you want to do. He was a murderer from the beginning, and does not stand in the truth, because there is no truth in him. When he speaks a lie, he speaks from his own resources, for he is a liar and the father of it. But because I tell the truth, you do not believe Me. Which of you convicts Me of sin? And if I tell the truth, why do you not believe Me? He who is of God hears God's words; therefore, you do not hear, because you are not of God."

Before Abraham Was, I AM

Then the Jews answered and said to Jesus, "Do we not say rightly that You are a Samaritan and have a demon?"

Jesus answered, "I do not have a demon; but I honour My Father, and you dishonour Me. And I do not seek My own glory; there is One who seeks and judges. I say to you, if anyone keeps My word he shall never see death."

Then the Jews said to Him, "Now we know that You have a demon! Abraham is dead, and the prophets; and You say, 'If anyone keeps My word he shall never taste death.' Are You greater than our father Abraham, who is dead? And the prophets are dead. Who do You make Yourself out to be?"

Jesus answered, "If I honour Myself, My honour is nothing. It is My Father who honours Me, of whom you say that He is your God. Yet you have not known Him, but I know Him. And if I say, 'I do not know Him,' I shall be a liar like you; but I do know Him and keep His word. Your father Abraham rejoiced to see My day, and he saw it and was glad."

Then the Jews said to Him, "You are not yet fifty years old, and have You seen Abraham?"

Jesus said to them, "I say to you, before Abraham was, I AM."

Then they took up stones to throw at Him; but Jesus hid Himself and went out of the temple, going through the middle of them, and went His way.

John 9:1-41

A Man Born Blind Receives Sight

Now as Jesus left the temple, He saw a man who was blind from birth. And His disciples asked Him, saying, "Rabbi, who sinned, this man or his parents, that he was born blind?"

Jesus answered, "Neither this man nor his parents sinned, but that the works of God should be revealed in him. I must work the works of Him who sent Me while it is day; the night is coming when no one can work. As long as I am in the world, I am the light of the world."

When Jesus had said these things, He spat on the ground and made clay with the saliva; and He anointed the eyes of the blind man with the clay. And Jesus said to him, "Go, wash in the pool of Siloam" (which is translated, Sent).

So, he went and washed, and came back seeing.

The neighbours and those who previously had seen that he was blind said, "Is not this the one who sat and begged?" Some said, "This is he." Others said, "He is like him."

The beggar replied, "I am he."

They said to him, "How were your eyes opened?"

The man who was healed answered and said, "A Man called Jesus made clay and anointed my eyes and said to me, 'Go to the pool of Siloam and wash.' So, I went and washed, and I received my sight."

Then they said to him, "Where is He?"

He said, "I do not know."

The Pharisees Excommunicate the Healed Man

The man's neighbours took him, who was previously blind, to the Pharisees.

Now it was a Sabbath when Jesus made the clay and opened his eyes. Then the Pharisees also asked the man again how he had received his sight.

He said to them, "He put clay on my eyes, and I washed, and I see."

Therefore, some of the Pharisees said, "This Man is not from God, because He does not keep the Sabbath."

Others said, "How can a man who is a sinner do such signs?" And there was a division among them.

They said to the man, who had his sight restored, tell us again, 'What do you say about Him because He opened your eyes?'"

He said, "He is a prophet."

But the Jews did not believe what he said, that he had been blind and received his sight.

Then the Pharisees called the parents of him who had received his sight. And they asked them, saying, "Is this your son, who you say was born blind? How then does he now see?"

His parents answered them and said, "We know that this is our son, and that he was born blind; but by what means he now sees we do not know, or who opened his eyes we do not know. He is of age; ask him. He will speak for himself." His parents said these things because they feared the Jews, for the Jews had agreed already that if anyone confessed that Jesus was Christ, they would be put out of the synagogue. For this reason, his parents said, "He is of age; ask him."

So, they again called the man who was blind, and said to him, "Give God the glory! We know that this Man is a sinner."

He answered and said, "Whether He is a sinner or not I do not know. One thing I know: that though I was blind, now I see."

Again, the Pharisees questioned him, "What did He do to you? How did He open your eyes?"

He replied to them, "I told you already, and you did not listen. Why do you want to hear it again? Do you also want to become His disciples?"

Then the Pharisees yelled at him and said, "You are His disciple, but we are Moses' disciples. We know that God spoke to Moses; as for this fellow, we do not know where He is from."

The man responded saying, "Why, this is a marvellous thing, that you do not know where He is from; yet, He has opened my eyes! Now we know that God does not hear sinners; but if anyone is a worshiper of God and does His will, He hears him. Since the world began it has been unheard of that anyone opened the eyes of one who was born blind. If this Man were not from God, He could do nothing."

The Pharisees answered and said to him, "You were completely born in sins, and are you teaching us?" And they threw him out of the temple.

True Vision and True Blindness

Jesus heard that they had thrown the healed man out; and when He had found him, He said to him, "Do you believe in the Son of God?"

He answered and said, "Who is He, Lord, that I may believe in Him?"

And Jesus said to him, "You have both seen Him and it is He who is talking with you."

Then he said, "Lord, I believe!" And he worshiped Him.

And Jesus said, "For judgment I have come into this world, that those who do not see may see, and that those who see may be made blind."

Then some of the Pharisees who were with Him heard these words, and said to Him, "Are we blind also?"

Jesus said to them, "If you were blind, you would have no sin; but now you say, 'We see.' Therefore, your sin remains.

John 10:1-21

Jesus the True Shepherd

"I say to you, he who does not enter the sheepfold by the door, but climbs up some other way, the same is a thief and a robber. But he who enters by the door is the shepherd of the sheep. To him the doorkeeper opens, and the sheep hear his voice; and he calls his own sheep by name and leads them out. And when he brings out his own sheep, he goes before them; and the sheep follow him, for they know his voice. But they will by no means follow a stranger, but will flee from him, for they do not know the voice of strangers."

Jesus used this illustration, but they did not understand the things which He spoke to them.

Jesus the Good Shepherd

Then Jesus said to them again, "I tell you, I am the door of the sheep. All who ever came before Me are thieves and robbers, but the sheep did not hear them. I am the door. If anyone enters by Me, he will be saved, and will go in and out and find pasture. The thief does not come except to steal, and to kill, and to destroy. I have come that they may have life, and that they may have it to the full.

"I am the good shepherd. The good shepherd gives His life for the sheep. But a hireling, he who is not the shepherd, one who does not own the sheep, sees the wolf coming and leaves the sheep and flees; and the wolf catches the sheep and scatters them. The hireling flees because he is a hireling and does not care about the sheep. I am the good shepherd; and I know My sheep, and am known by My own. As the Father knows Me, even so I know the Father; and I lay down My life for the sheep. And other sheep I have which are not of this fold; them also I must bring, and they will hear My voice; and there will be one flock and one shepherd.

"My Father loves Me, because I lay down My life that I may take it again. No one takes it from Me, but I lay it down of Myself. I have power to lay it down, and I have power to take it again. This command I have received from My Father."

Then there was a division again among the Jews because of these sayings. And many of them said, "He has a demon and is mad. Why do you listen to Him?" Others said, "These are not the words of one who has a demon. Can a demon open the eyes of the blind?"

Matthew 8:18-22, Luke 9:57-62

The Cost of Discipleship

Now it happened, as Jesus and His followers journeyed on the road, Jesus saw great multitudes about Him so, He gave a command to depart to the other side.

Then a certain scribe came and said to Him, "Teacher, I will follow You wherever You go."

And Jesus said to him, "Foxes have holes and birds of the air have nests, but the Son of Man has nowhere to lay His head."

Then another of His disciples said to Him, "Lord, let me first go and bury my father."

But Jesus said to him, "Follow Me, and let the dead bury their own dead. You go and preach the kingdom of God."

And another also said, "Lord, I will follow You, but let me first go and bid them farewell who are at my house."

But Jesus said to him, "No one, having put his hand to the plow, and looking back, is fit for the kingdom of God."

Luke 9:51-56

A Samaritan Village Rejects the Saviour

Now it came to pass, when the time had come for Him to be received up, Jesus steadfastly set His face to go to Jerusalem, and sent messengers before Him.

And as they went, they entered a village of the Samaritans, to prepare for Him. But they did not receive Him, because His face was set for the journey to Jerusalem. And when His disciples James and John saw this, they said, "Lord, do You want us to command fire to come down from heaven and consume them, just as Elijah did?"

But He turned and rebuked them, and said, "You do not know what manner of spirit you are of. For the Son of Man did not come to destroy men's lives but to save them."

And they went to another village.

Matthew 11:20-24, Luke 10:13-16

Woe to the Impenitent Cities

Then Jesus began to rebuke the cities in which most of His mighty works had been done, because they did not repent. "Woe to you, Chorazin! Woe to you, Bethsaida! For if the mighty works which were done in you had been done in Tyre and Sidon, they would have repented long ago, sitting in sackcloth and ashes. But I say to you, it will be more tolerable for Tyre and Sidon at the day of judgment than for you. And you, Capernaum, who are exalted to heaven, will be brought down to Hades; for if the mighty works which were done in you had been done in Sodom, it would have remained until this day. But I say to you that it shall be more tolerable for the land of Sodom in the day of judgment than for you. He who hears you hears Me, he who rejects you rejects Me, and he who rejects Me rejects Him who sent Me."

Luke 10:1-12, 17-20

The Seventy Sent Out

After these things, the Lord appointed seventy others also, and sent them out, two by two before Him into every city and place where He Himself was about to go.

Then He said to them, "The harvest truly is great, but the labourers are few; therefore, pray the Lord of the harvest to send out labourers into His harvest. Go your way; I send you out as lambs among wolves. Carry neither money bag, knapsack, or sandals; and greet no one along the road. But whatever house you enter, first say, 'Peace to this house.' And if a son of peace is there, your peace will rest on it; if not, it will return to you. And remain in the same house, eating and drinking such things as they give, for the labourer is worthy of his wages. Do not go from house to house. And heal the sick there, and say to them, 'The kingdom of God has come near to you.' But whatever city you enter, and they do not receive you, go out into its streets and say, 'The dust of your city which clings to us we wipe off against you. Know this, that the kingdom of God has come near to you.' But I say to you that it will be more tolerable in that Day for Sodom than for that city."

The Seventy Return with Joy

Then the seventy returned with joy, saying, "Lord, even the demons are subject to us in Your name."

And He said to them, "I saw Satan fall like lightning from heaven. I give you the authority to trample on serpents and scorpions, and over all the power of the enemy, and nothing shall by any means hurt you. Do not rejoice in this, that the spirits are subject to you, but rather rejoice because your names are written in heaven."

Matthew 11:25-30, Luke 10:21-24

Jesus Rejoices in the Spirit

In that hour Jesus rejoiced in the Spirit and said, "I thank You, Father, Lord of heaven and earth, that You have hidden these things from the wise, but showed care and thought for the future, and revealed them to babes, for Father, it seemed good in Your sight."

Jesus said, "All things have been delivered to Me by My Father, and no one knows who the Son is except the Father, and who the Father is except the Son, and the one to whom the Son wills to reveal Him."

Jesus Gives True Rest

Then Jesus turned to His disciples and said privately, "Come to Me, all you who labour and are heavy laden, and I will give you rest. Take My yoke upon you and learn from Me, for I am gentle and lowly in heart, and you will find rest for your souls. For My yoke is easy and My burden is light. Blessed are the eyes which see the things you see; for I tell you that many prophets and kings have desired to see what you see, and have not seen it, and to hear what you hear, and have not heard it."

Luke 10:25-37

The Parable of the Good Samaritan

And Jesus observed a certain lawyer stood up to test Him, saying, "Teacher, what shall I do to inherit eternal life?"

Jesus said to him, "What is written in the law? How do you understand the law?"

So, he answered and said, "*You shall love the Lord your God with all your heart, with all your soul, with all your strength, and with all your mind,'* and *'your neighbour as yourself.'*"

And Jesus said to him, "You have answered correctly; do this and you will live."

But the lawyer, wanting to justify himself, said to Jesus, "And who is my neighbour?"

Then Jesus answered and said: "A certain man went down from Jerusalem to Jericho, and fell among thieves, who stripped him of his clothing, wounded him, and departed, leaving him half dead. Now by chance a certain priest came down that road. And when he saw him, he moved over to the other side. When a Levite arrived at the place, he came and looked, and walked by on the other side. But a certain Samaritan, as he journeyed, came and knelt down by the wounded man. And when he saw how badly he had been treated, had compassion on him. He bandaged his wounds, pouring on oil and wine. He sat him on his own animal, brought him to an inn, and took care of him. On the next day, when the Samaritan departed, he took out two denarii, gave them to the innkeeper, and said to him, 'Take care of this man; whatever more you spend, when I come again, I will repay you.' So, which of these three do you think was neighbour to him who was beaten and robbed by the thieves?"

And he said, "He who showed mercy on him."

Then Jesus said to him, "Go and do likewise."

Luke 10:38-42

Mary and Martha Worship and Serve

Now it happened as Jesus and His disciples continued, they entered a certain village; and a woman named Martha welcomed Jesus into her house. And she had a sister called Mary, who also sat at Jesus' feet and heard His word. But Martha was distracted with much serving, and she approached Him and said, "Lord, do You not care that my sister has left me to serve alone? Please tell her to help me."

And Jesus answered and said to her, "Martha, Martha, you are worried and troubled about many things. But one thing is needed, and Mary has chosen that good part, which will not be taken away from her."

Luke 11:37 to 12:12

Woe to the Pharisees and Lawyers

And as Jesus spoke, a certain Pharisee asked Him to dine with him. So, He went in and sat down to eat. When the Pharisee saw it, he marvelled that He had not first washed before dinner.

Then the Lord said to him, "Now you Pharisees make the outside of the cup and dish clean, but your inward part is full of greed and wickedness. Foolish ones! Did not He who made the outside make the inside also? But rather give money of such things as you have; then all things are clean to you.

"But woe to you Pharisees! For you tithe mint and rue and all manner of herbs, and pass by justice and the love of God. These you should have done, without leaving the others undone. Woe to you Pharisees! For you love the best seats in the synagogues and greetings in the marketplaces. Woe to you, scribes and Pharisees, hypocrites! For you are like graves which are not seen, and the men who walk over them are not aware of them."

Then one of the lawyers answered and said to Him, "Teacher, by saying these things You offend us also."

And He said, "Woe to you also, lawyers! For you load men with burdens hard to bear, and you yourselves do not touch the burdens with one of your fingers. Woe to you! For you build the tombs of the prophets, and your fathers killed them. In fact, you accept the witness and you approve the deeds of your fathers; for they killed them, and you build their tombs. The wisdom of God also said, 'I will send them prophets and apostles, and some of them they will kill and persecute, that the blood of all the prophets which was given from the foundation of the world may be required of this generation, from the blood of Abel to the blood of Zechariah who perished between the altar and the temple.' Yes, I say to you, it shall be required of this generation. Woe to you lawyers! For you have taken away the key of knowledge. You did not enter in yourselves, and those who were entering in you hindered."

And as He said these things to them, the scribes and the Pharisees began to question Him angrily, and to cross-examine Him about many things, lying in wait for Him, and trying to catch Him in something He might say, that they might accuse Him.

Beware of Hypocrisy

In the meantime, when an innumerable multitude of people had gathered together, so that they trampled one another, Jesus began to say to His disciples first of all, "Beware of the leaven of the Pharisees, which is hypocrisy. For there is nothing covered that will not be revealed, or hidden that will not be known. Therefore, whatever you have spoken in the dark will be heard in the light, and what you have spoken in the ear in inner rooms will be proclaimed on the housetops.

Jesus Teaches the Fear of God

"And I say to you, My friends, do not be afraid of those who kill the body, and after that have no more that they can do to you. But I will show you whom you should fear: Fear Him who, after He has killed, has power to cast into hell; yes, I say to you, fear Him!

"Are not five sparrows sold for two copper coins? And not one of them is forgotten before God. But the very hairs of your head are all numbered. Do not fear, because you are of more value than many sparrows.

Confess Christ Before Men

"Also, I say to you, whoever confesses Me before men, him the Son of Man also will confess before the angels of God.

"But he who denies Me before men will be denied before the angels of God. And anyone who speaks a word against the Son of Man, it will be forgiven him; but to him who blasphemes against the Holy Spirit, it will not be forgiven.

"Now when they bring you to the synagogues and magistrates and authorities, do not worry about how or what you should answer, or what you should say. For the Holy Spirit will teach you in that very hour what you need to say."

Luke 12:13-21

The Parable of the Rich Fool

Then one from the crowd said to Him, "Teacher, tell my brother to divide the inheritance with me."

But Jesus said to him, "Man, who made Me a judge or an arbitrator over you?"

And He said to them, "Take heed and beware of covetousness, for one's life does not consist in the abundance of the things he possesses."

Then He spoke a parable to them, saying: "The ground of a certain rich man yielded plentifully. And he thought within himself, saying, 'What shall I do, since I have no room to store my crops?' So, he said, 'I will do this: I will pull down my barns and build larger barns, and there I will store all my crops and my goods. And I will say to my soul, "Soul, you have many goods stored up for many years; take your ease; eat, drink, and be merry." "But God said to him, 'Fool! This night your soul will be required of you; then whose will those things be which you have provided?'

"So is he who lays up treasure for himself, and is not rich toward God."

Luke 12:35-59

The Faithful Servant and the Evil Servant

"Wear a belt around your waist and your lamps burning; and you, be like men who wait for their master, when he returns from the wedding. When he comes and knocks, you are ready and open to him immediately. Blessed are those servants who the master, when he comes, will find watching. I say to you, that he will put on his belt and have them sit down to eat, and will come and serve them. And if he should come in the second watch, or come in the third watch, and find them so, blessed are those servants. But know this, that if the master of the house had known what hour the thief would come, he would have watched and not allowed his house to be broken into. You also be ready, for the Son of Man is coming at an hour you do not expect."

Then Peter said to Him, "Lord, do You speak this parable only to us, or to all people?"

And the Lord said, "Who then is that faithful and wise steward, who his master will make ruler over his household, to give them their portion of food in due season? Blessed is that servant who his master will find so doing when he comes. I tell you the truth, he will make him ruler over all that he has. But if that servant says in his heart, 'My master is delaying his coming,' and begins to beat the male and female servants, and to eat and drink and be drunk, the master of that servant will come on a day when he is not looking for him, and at an hour when he is not aware, and will cut him in two and appoint him his portion with the unbelievers. And that servant who knew his master's will, and did not prepare himself or do according to his will, shall be beaten with many stripes. But he who did not know, yet committed things deserving of stripes, shall be beaten with few. For everyone to whom much is given, from him much will be required; and to whom much has been committed, of him they will ask the more.

Christ Brings Division

"I came to send fire on the earth, and how I wish it were already kindled! But I have a baptism to be baptized with, and how distressed I am till it is accomplished! Do you suppose that I came to give peace on earth? I tell you, not at all, but rather division. For from now on five in one house will be divided: three against two, and two against three. Father will be divided against son and son against father, mother against daughter and daughter against mother, mother-in-law against her daughter-in-law and daughter-in-law against her mother-in-law."

Discern the Time

Then Jesus also said to the multitudes, "Whenever you see a cloud rising out of the west, immediately you say, 'A shower is coming'; and so, it is. And when you see the south wind blow, you say, 'There will be hot weather'; and there is. Hypocrites! You can discern the face of the sky and of the earth, but how is It you do not discern this time?

Make Peace with Your Adversary

"Yes, and why, even of yourselves, do you not judge what is right? When you go with your adversary to the magistrate, make every effort along the way to settle with him, otherwise he drag you to the judge, the judge deliver you to the officer, and the officer throw you into prison. I tell you, you shall not depart from there until you have paid the very last part of all you owe."

Luke 13:1-9

Repent or Perish

There were present at that season some who told Him about the Galileans whose blood Pilate had mingled with their sacrifices. And Jesus answered and said to them, "Do you suppose that these Galileans were worse sinners than all other Galileans, because they suffered such things? I tell you, no; but unless you repent you will all perish. Or those eighteen on whom the tower in Siloam fell and killed them, do you think that they were worse sinners than all other men who dwelt in Jerusalem? I tell you, no; but unless you repent you will all perish as they did."

The Parable of the Barren Fig Tree

Jesus also spoke this parable: "A certain man had a fig tree planted in his vineyard, and he came seeking fruit on it and found none. Then he said to the keeper of his vineyard, 'Look, for three years I have come looking for fruit on this fig tree and find none. Cut it down; why does it use up the ground?' But the keeper answered and said to him, 'Sir, let it grow for another year. I will dig around it and fertilize it. And if next year, it gives you fruit, good. But if not, after that you can cut it down.'"

Luke 13:10-17

A Spirit of Infirmity

Now Jesus was teaching in one of the synagogues on the Sabbath. Inside, there was a woman who had a spirit of infirmity eighteen years, and was bent over and could in no way stand up straight.

But when Jesus saw her, He called her to Him and said to her, "Woman, you are loosed from your infirmity." And He laid His hands on her, and immediately she was made straight, and glorified God.

But the ruler of the synagogue answered angrily as he was annoyed because Jesus had healed on the Sabbath; and he said to the crowd, "There are six days on which men ought to work; come and be healed on them, and not on the Sabbath day."

The Lord then answered him and said, "Hypocrite! Does not each one of you on the Sabbath loose his ox or donkey from the stall, and lead it away to water it? Think of this! Should not this woman, being a daughter of Abraham, whom Satan has bound for eighteen years, be set free from this bond on the Sabbath?"

And when He said these things, all those who objected to what Jesus did, were put to shame; and all the multitude rejoiced for all the glorious things that were done by Him.

Luke 13:22-35

The Narrow Way

And Jesus went through the cities and villages, teaching, and journeying toward Jerusalem.

Then one said to Him, "Lord, are there few who are saved?"

And He said to them, "Make sure you enter through the narrow gate, for many, I say to you, will seek to enter and will not be able. When once the Master of the house has risen up and shut the door, and you begin to stand outside and knock at the door, saying, 'Lord, Lord, open for us,' He will answer and say to you, 'I do not know you, or where you are from,' then you will begin to say, 'We ate and drank in Your presence, and You taught in our streets.' But He will say, 'I tell you I do not know you, or where you are from. Depart from Me, all you workers of iniquity.' There will be weeping and gnashing of teeth, when you see Abraham and Isaac and Jacob and all the prophets in the kingdom of God, and yourselves thrown out. They will come from the east and the west, from the north and the south, and sit down in the kingdom of God. And indeed, there are last who will be first, and there are first who will be last."

On that very day some Pharisees came, saying to Him, "Get out and depart from here, for Herod wants to kill You."

And He said to them, "Go, tell that fox, 'Let him see, I cast out demons and perform cures today and tomorrow, and the third day I shall be made perfect.' Now, I must journey today, tomorrow, and the day following; for it cannot be that a prophet should perish outside of Jerusalem.

Jesus Laments over Jerusalem

"O Jerusalem, Jerusalem, the one who kills the prophets and stones those who are sent to her! How often I wanted to gather your children together, as a hen gathers her brood under her wings, but you were not willing! See! Your house is left to you desolate; and I say to you, you shall not see Me until the time comes when you say, 'Blessed is He who comes in the name of the Lord!'"

Luke 14:1-24

A Man with Dropsy Healed on the Sabbath

Now it happened, as Jesus went into the house of one of the rulers of the Pharisees to eat bread on the Sabbath, that the lawyers and the Pharisees watched Him closely. And Jesus noticed, there was a certain man before Him who had dropsy. And Jesus, answering, spoke to the lawyers and Pharisees, saying, "Is it lawful to heal on the Sabbath?"

But they kept silent. And He took him and healed him, and let him go.

Then He answered them, saying, "Which of you, having a donkey or an ox that has fallen into a pit, will not immediately pull him out on the Sabbath day?" And they could not answer Him regarding these things.

Take the Lowly Place

Jesus told a parable to those who were invited, when He noted how they chose the best places, saying to them: "When you are invited by anyone to a wedding feast, do not sit down in the best place, in case one more honourable than you be invited by him; and he who invited you and him come and say to you, 'Give place to this man,' and then you, with shame, take the lowest place. But when you are invited, go and sit down in the lowest place, so that when he who invited you comes he may say to you, 'Friend, go up higher.' Then you will have glory in the presence of those who sit at the table with you. For whoever exalts himself will be humbled, and he who humbles himself will be exalted."

Then He also said to him who invited Him, "When you give a dinner or a supper, do not ask your friends, your brothers, your relatives, or rich neighbours, because they will feel obliged to invite you back, and you be repaid. But when you give a feast, invite the poor, the maimed, the lame, the blind. And you will be blessed, because they cannot repay you; for you shall be repaid at the resurrection of the just."

The Parable of the Great Supper

Now when one of those who sat at the table with Jesus heard these things, he said to Him, "Blessed is he who shall eat bread in the kingdom of God!"

Then He said to him, "A certain man gave a great supper and invited many, and sent his servant at supper time to say to those who were invited, 'Come, for all things are now ready.' But they all began to make excuses. The first said to him, 'I have bought a piece of ground, and I must go and see it. I ask you to have me excused.' And another said, 'I have bought five yoke of oxen, and I am going to test them. I ask you to have me excused.' Still another said, 'I have married a wife, and therefore I cannot come.' So that servant came and reported these things to his master. Then the master of the house, being angry, said to his servant, 'Go out quickly into the streets and lanes of the city, and bring in here the poor and the maimed and the lame and the blind.' And the servant said, 'Master, it is done as you commanded, and still there is room.' Then the master said to the servant, 'Go out into the highways and hedges, and compel them to come in, that my house may be filled. For I say to you that none of those men who were invited shall taste my supper.'"

Luke 14:25-35

Leaving All to Follow Christ

Now great multitudes went with Jesus. And He turned and said to them, "If anyone comes to Me and does not hate his father and mother, wife and children, brothers and sisters, yes, and his own life also, he cannot be My disciple. And whoever does not bear his cross and come after Me cannot be My disciple. For which of you, intending to build a tower, does not sit down first and count the cost, whether he has enough to finish it in case, after he has laid the foundation, and is not able to finish, all who see it begin to tease him, saying, 'This man began to build and was not able to finish'? Or what king, going to make war against another king, does not sit down first and consider whether he is able with ten thousand to meet him who comes against him with twenty thousand? Or else, while the other is still a great way off, he sends a delegation and asks conditions of peace. I say to you, "Whoever of you does not leave all that he has, cannot be My disciple."

Tasteless Salt Is Worthless

Jesus continued, "Salt is good; but if the salt has lost its flavour, how shall it be seasoned? It is neither fit for the land nor for the rubbish heap, but men throw it out. He who has ears to hear, let him hear!

Matthew 18:10-14, Luke 15:1-32

The Parable of the Lost Sheep

"Listen, that you do not despise one of these little ones, for I say to you that in heaven their angels always see the face of My Father who is in heaven. For the Son of Man has come to save that which was lost."

Then all the tax collectors and the sinners came near to Jesus to hear Him. And the Pharisees and scribes complained, saying, "This Man receives sinners and eats with them."

So, He spoke this parable to them, saying: "What man of you, having a hundred sheep, if he loses one of them or one goes astray into the mountains, does not leave the ninety-nine in the wilderness, and go after the one which is lost until he finds it? And when he has found it, he lays it on his shoulders, rejoicing. And when he comes home, he calls together his friends and neighbours, saying to them, 'Rejoice with me, for I have found my sheep which was lost!' I say to you, he rejoices more over that sheep than over the ninety-nine that did not go astray. I say to you, there will be more joy in heaven over one sinner who repents than over ninety-nine just persons who need no repentance. Even so, it is not the will of your Father who is in heaven that one of these little ones should perish.

The Parable of the Lost Coin

"Or what woman, having ten silver coins, if she loses one coin, does not light a lamp, sweep the house, and search carefully until she finds it? And when she has found it, she calls her friends and neighbours together, saying, 'Rejoice with me, for I have found the piece which I lost!' Again, I say to you, "There is joy in the presence of the angels of God over one sinner who repents.'"

The Parable of the Lost Son

Then Jesus said, "A certain man had two sons. And the younger of them said to his father, 'Father, give me the portion of goods that belongs to me.' So, he divided to them all his possessions. And a few days after, the younger son gathered all together, journeyed to a far country, and there wasted his possessions with prodigal living. But when he had spent all, a severe famine came in that land, and he began to be in want. Then he went and worked for a citizen of that country, and he sent him into his fields to feed pigs. And he would gladly have filled his stomach with the pods that the pigs ate, and no one gave him anything.

"But then the thought came to him, 'How many of my father's hired servants have bread enough and to spare, and I perish with hunger! I will leave and go to my father, and say to him, 'Father, I have sinned against heaven and before you, and I am no longer worthy to be called your son. Make me like one of your hired servants.' And he left and came to his father.

"But when he was still a great way off, his father saw him and had compassion, and ran and fell on his neck and kissed him. And the son said to him, 'Father, I have sinned against heaven and in your sight, and am no longer worthy to be called your son.'

"But the father said to his servants, 'Bring out the best robe and put it on him, and put a ring on his hand and sandals on his feet. And bring the fatted calf here and kill it, and let us eat and be merry; for this my son was dead and is alive again; he was lost and is found.' And they began to celebrate.

"Now his older son was in the field. And as he came and approached near to the house, he heard music and dancing. So, he called one of the servants and asked what these things meant. And he said to him, 'Your brother has returned home, and because your father has received him safe and sound, he has killed the fatted calf.'

"But the older son was angry and would not go in. His father came out and pleaded with him to come in.

"But, he answered and said to his father, 'All these many years I have been serving you; I never broken your commandment at any time; and yet you never gave me a young goat, that I might make merry with my friends. But as soon as this son of yours came, who has devoured your livelihood with harlots, you killed the fatted calf for him.'

"And he said to him, 'Son, you are always with me, and all that I have is yours. It was right that we should celebrate and be glad, for your brother was dead and is alive again. He was lost and is found.'"

Luke 16:1-31

The Parable of the Unjust Steward

Then Jesus said to His disciples: "There was a certain rich man who had a manager, and a complaint was brought to him that this man was wasting his goods. So, he called the manager and said to him, 'What is this I hear about you? Give me an account of your ability to manage my possessions, for you are no longer fit to be my manager.'

"Then the manager said to himself, 'What shall I do? For my employer is taking the manager-ship away from me. I cannot dig; I am ashamed to beg. I know what to do, that when I am put out of my employment, they may receive me into their houses.'

"So, he called every one of his employer's debtors, and said to the first, 'How much do you owe my employer?' And he said, 'A hundred measures of oil.' So, he said to him, 'Take your bill, and sit down quickly and write fifty.' Then he said to another, 'And how much do you owe?' So, he said, 'A hundred measures of wheat.' And he said to him, 'Take your bill, and write eighty.' So, the rich man commended his manager because he had used good management to those who owed him. For the sons of this world are more shrewd in their generation than the sons of light.

"And I say to you, make friends for yourselves by unrighteous men, that when you fail, they may receive you into an everlasting home. He who is faithful in what is small, is also faithful in much; and he who is unfaithful in what is small is also unfaithful in much. If you have not been faithful to the unrighteous man, who will need to trust you with their true riches? And if you have not been faithful in what is another man's, who will give you what is your own?

"No servant can serve two masters; for either he will hate the one and love the other, or else he will be loyal to the one and despise the other. You cannot serve God and man."

The Law, the Prophets, and the Kingdom

Now the Pharisees, who were lovers of money, also heard all these things, and they ridiculed Him.

And Jesus said to them, "You justify your selves before men, but God knows your hearts. For what is highly esteemed among men is a disgustful thing in the sight of God.

"The law and the prophets were until John. Since that time the kingdom of God has been preached, and everyone is wanting answers now. And it is easier for heaven and earth to pass away than for one jot or tittle of the law to fail. Whoever divorces his wife and marries another commits adultery; and whoever marries her who is divorced from her husband commits adultery."

The Rich Man and Lazarus

Then Jesus said, "There was a certain rich man who was clothed in purple and fine linen and ate sumptuously every day. But there was a certain beggar named Lazarus, full of sores, who was laid at his gate, desiring to be fed with the crumbs which fell from the rich man's table. Besides, the dogs came and licked his sores.

So, it was that the beggar died, and was carried by the angels to the arms of Abraham. The rich man also died and was buried. And being tormented in Hades, he lifted up his eyes and saw Abraham in the distance, and Lazarus in his arms.

"Then the rich man yelled out and said, 'Father Abraham, have mercy on me, and send Lazarus that he may dip the tip of his finger in water and cool my tongue; for I am tormented in this flame.'

"But Abraham said, 'Son, remember that in your lifetime you received your good things, and likewise Lazarus evil things; but now he is comforted and you are tormented. And besides all this, between us and you there is a great gulf fixed, so that those who want to pass from here to you cannot, nor can those from there pass to us.'

"The rich man said, 'I beg you therefore, father, that you would send Lazarus to my father's house, for I have five brothers, that he may testify to them, in case they also come to this place of torment.'

"Abraham said to him, 'They have Moses and the prophets; let them hear them.'

"The rich man replied, 'No, father Abraham; but if one goes to them from the dead, they will repent.'

"But Abraham said to him, 'If they do not hear Moses and the prophets, neither will they be persuaded though one rise from the dead.'"

Matthew 18:15-35, Luke 17:1-10

Dealing with a Sinning Brother

Jesus continued. "If your brother sins against you, go and tell him his fault between you and him alone. If he hears you, you have gained your brother. But if he will not hear, take with you one or two more, that *'by the mouth of two or three witnesses every word may be established.'* And if he refuses to hear them, tell it to the church. But if he refuses even to hear the church, let him be to you like a heathen and a tax collector.

"I say to you, whatever you bind on earth will be bound in heaven, and whatever you loose on earth will be loosed in heaven.

"Again, I say to you that if two of you agree on earth concerning anything that they ask, it will be done for them by My Father in heaven. For where two or three are gathered together in My name, I am there in the middle of them."

The Parable of the Unforgiving Servant

Then Peter came to Him and said, "Lord, how often shall my brother sin against me, and I forgive him? Up to seven times?"

Jesus said to him, "I do not say to you, up to seven times, but up to seventy times seven. I say to you; the kingdom of heaven is like a certain king who wanted to settle accounts with his servants. And when he had begun to settle accounts, one was brought to him who owed him ten thousand talents. But as he was not able to pay, his master commanded that he be sold, with his wife and children and all that he had, and that payment be made. The servant therefore fell down before him, saying, 'Master, have patience with me, and I will pay you all.' Then the master of that servant was moved with compassion, released him, and forgave him the debt.

"But that servant went out and found one of his fellow servants who owed him a hundred denarii; and he laid hands on him and took him by the throat, saying, 'Pay me what you owe!' So, his fellow servant fell down at his feet and begged him, saying, 'Have patience with me, and I will pay you all.' And he would not, but went and threw him into prison till he should pay the debt. So, when the other servants saw what had been done, they were very angry, and came and told their master all that had been done. Then his master, after he had called him, said to him, 'You wicked servant! I forgave you all that debt because you begged me. Should you not also have had compassion on your fellow servant, just as I had pity on you?' And his master was very angry, and delivered him to the torturers until he should pay all that was due to him.

"So, My heavenly Father also will do to you if each of you, from his heart, does not forgive his brother his offences."

Jesus Warns of Offenses

Then Jesus said to the disciples, "It is impossible that no offenses should come, but woe to him through whom they do come! It would be better for him if a millstone were hung around his neck, and he were thrown into the sea, than that he should offend one of these little ones. Take note to yourselves. If your brother sins against you, rebuke him; and if he repents, forgive him. And if he sins against you seven times in a day, and seven times in a day returns to you, saying, 'I repent,' you shall forgive him."

Faith and Duty

And the apostles said to the Lord, "Increase our faith."

So, the Lord said, "If you have faith as a mustard seed, you can say to this mulberry tree, 'Be pulled up by the roots and be planted in the sea,' and it would obey you. And which of you, having a servant ploughing or looking after sheep, will say to him when he has come in from the field, 'Come at once and sit down to eat'? But will he not rather say to him, 'Prepare something for my supper. Put your belt on yourself and serve me till I have eaten and drunk, and afterward you will eat and drink'? Does he thank that servant because he did the things that were commanded him? I think not.

So, I say, when you have done all those things which you are commanded, say, 'We are unprofitable servants. We have done what was our duty to do.'"

Luke 17:11-19

Ten Lepers Cleansed

Now it happened as Jesus went to Jerusalem that He passed through the midst of Samaria and Galilee.

Then as He entered a certain village, there met Him ten men who were lepers, who stood at a distance. And they shouted out loudly with their voices and said, "Jesus, Master, have mercy on us!"

So, when He saw them, He said to them, "Go, show yourselves to the priests." And so it was, that as they went, they were healed.

And one of them, when he saw that he was healed, returned, and with a loud voice glorified God, and fell down on his face at His feet, giving Him thanks. And he was a Samaritan.

So, Jesus answered and said, "Were there not ten healed? But where are the nine? Were there not any found who returned to give glory to God except this foreigner?" And He said to him, "Stand up and go your way. Your faith has made you well."

Luke 17:20-37

The Coming of the Kingdom

Now when Jesus was asked by the Pharisees when the kingdom of God would come, He answered them and said, "The kingdom of God does not come with observation; or will they say, 'See here!' or 'See there!' For the kingdom of God is within you."

Then He said to the disciples, "The days will come when you will desire to see one of the days of the Son of Man, and you will not see it. And they will say to you, 'Look here!' or 'Look there!' Do not go after them or follow them. For as the lightning that flashes out of one part under heaven shines to the other part under heaven, so also the Son of Man will be in His day. But first He must suffer many things and be rejected by this generation. And as it was in the days of Noah, so it will be also in the days of the Son of Man: They ate, they drank, they married wives, they were given in marriage, until the day that Noah entered the ark, and the flood came and destroyed them all. It will be the same way, as it was also in the days of Lot: They ate, they drank, they bought, they sold, they planted, they built; but on the day that Lot went out of Sodom it rained fire and brimstone from heaven and destroyed them all. Even so will it be in the day when the Son of Man is revealed.

"In that day, he who is on the housetop, and his goods are in the house, let him not come down to take them away. Also, the one who is in the field, let him not turn back. Remember Lot's wife. Whoever seeks to save his life will lose it, and whoever loses his life will preserve it. I tell you, in that night there will be two men in one bed: the one will be taken and the other will be left. Two women will be grinding together: the one will be taken and the other left. Two men will be in the field: the one will be taken and the other left."

And they answered and said to Him, "Where, Lord?"

So, He said to them, "Wherever the body is, there the eagles will be gathered together."

Luke 18:1-14

The Parable of the Persistent Widow

Then Jesus spoke a parable to them, that men should always pray and not lose heart, saying: "There was in a certain city a judge who did not fear God or regarded man. Now there was a widow in that city; and she came to him, saying, 'Get justice for me from this one who is taking advantage of me.' And he would not for a while; but afterward he said within himself, 'Though I do not fear God or regard man, but because this widow troubles me I will give her what she asks, unless by her continual coming she tires me out.'"

Then the Lord said, "Hear what the unjust judge said. And shall God not listen and give to His own people, who cry out day and night to Him, though He endures for a long time with them? I tell you that He will grant their request speedily.

But I say, 'When the Son of Man comes, will He really find faith on the earth?'"

The Parable of the Pharisee and the Tax Collector

Also, Jesus spoke this parable to some who trusted in themselves that they were righteous, and despised others. "Two men went up to the temple to pray, one a Pharisee and the other a tax collector. The Pharisee stood and prayed with himself, 'God, I thank You that I am not like other men, extortioners, unjust, adulterers, or even as this tax collector. I fast twice a week; I give tithes of all that I possess.' And the tax collector, standing at a distance, would not so much as raise his eyes to heaven, but showed signs of sorrow, despair and regret, saying, 'God, be merciful to me a sinner!' I tell you, this man went down to his house justified rather than the other; for everyone who lifts themselves up will be brought down, and he who humbles himself will be exalted."

Matthew 19:1-15, Mark 10:1-16, Luke 18:15-17

Marriage and Divorce

When Jesus had finished these sayings, He and His disciples departed from Galilee and came to the region of Judea by the other side of Jordan. And great multitudes gathered and followed Him, and He healed them there.

As He was accustomed, He taught them as well. The Pharisees also came to Him, testing Him, and saying to Him, "Is it lawful for a man to divorce his wife for just any reason?"

And He answered and said to them, "What did Moses command you?"

They said, "Moses permitted a man to write a certificate of divorce, and to dismiss her."

And Jesus answered and said to them, "Because of the hardness of your heart he wrote you this general rule. Have you not read that

He who made them at the beginning made them male and female? For this reason, a man shall leave his father and mother and be joined to his wife, and the two shall become one flesh'. They are no longer two but one flesh. I say to you, what God has joined together, let no man separate. And I say to you, whoever divorces his wife, except for sexual immorality, and marries another, commits adultery; and whoever marries her who is divorced commits adultery."

In the house, His disciples also asked Him again about the same matter.

He said to them, "Whoever divorces his wife and marries another commits adultery against her. And if a woman divorces her husband and marries another, she commits adultery."

His disciples said to Him, "If such is the case of the man with his wife, it is better not to marry."

Jesus Teaches on Celibacy

But Jesus said to them, "All cannot accept this saying, but only those to whom it has been given: For there are eunuchs who were born from their mother's womb, and there are eunuchs who were made eunuchs by men, and there are eunuchs who have made themselves eunuchs for the kingdom of heaven's sake. He who is able to accept it, let him accept it."

Jesus Blesses Little Children

Then little children were brought to Jesus that He might put His hands on them and pray, but when the disciples saw it, they sent them away.

But when Jesus saw it, He was greatly displeased and called them to Him and said, "Let the little children come to Me, and do not stop them; for of such is the kingdom of God. I say to you, whoever does not receive the kingdom of God as a little child will by no means enter it."

And He took them up in His arms, laid His hands on them, and blessed them, and after this they departed from there.

Matthew 19:16-30, Mark 10:17-31, Luke 18:18-30

Jesus Counsels the Rich Young Ruler

Now as Jesus was going out on the road, a certain ruler came running, knelt before Him, and asked Him, "Good Teacher, what shall I do that I may inherit eternal life?"

Jesus said to him, "Why do you call Me good? No one is good but One, that is, God. But if you want to enter into life, keep the commandments."

He said to Him, "Which ones?"

Jesus said, "'Do not commit adultery,' 'Do not murder,' 'Do not steal,' 'Do not bear false witness,' 'Honour your father and your mother,' and, 'You shall love your neighbour as yourself.'"

And he answered and said to Him, "Teacher, all these things I have kept from my youth." What do I still lack?"

When Jesus heard these things, He looked at him and loved him.

He said to him, "If you want to be perfect, go, sell all you have and distribute to the poor, and you will have treasure in heaven; and come, take up your cross and follow Me."

But when the young man heard this, he became very sad and sorrowful at this word, for he was very rich, and had great possessions.

Jesus said to them, "I say to you, everyone who has left houses or brothers or sisters or father or mother or wife or children or lands, for My name's sake, shall receive a hundredfold, and inherit eternal life. But many who are first will be last, and the last first."

With God All Things Are Possible

And when Jesus saw that he became very sorrowful, He looked around and said to His disciples, "I say to you that it is hard for a rich man to enter the kingdom of heaven. And again, I say to you, it is easier for a camel to go through the eye of a needle than for a rich man to enter the kingdom of God."

When His disciples heard it, they were greatly astonished at His words.

And those who heard it said, "Who then can be saved?"

But Jesus answered again and said to them, "Children, how hard it is for those who trust in riches to enter the kingdom of God!"

Then Jesus looked at them and said, "With men it is impossible, but not with God; for with God all things are possible."

Then Peter said to Him, "See, we have left all and followed You. Therefore, what shall we have?"

Jesus answered and said, "I say to you, that in the regeneration, when the Son of Man sits on the throne of His glory, you who have followed Me will also sit on twelve thrones, judging the twelve tribes of Israel. There is no one who has left house or brothers or sisters or father or mother or wife or children or lands, for My sake and the gospel's, who shall not receive a hundredfold now in this time, houses and brothers and sisters and mothers and children and lands, with persecutions, and in the age to come, eternal life. But many who are first will be last, and the last first.

Matthew 20:1-16

The Parable of the Workers in the Vineyard

"For the kingdom of heaven is like a landowner who went out early in the morning to hire labourers for his vineyard.

"Now when he had agreed with the labourers for a denarius a day, he sent them into his vineyard. And he went out about the third hour and saw others standing idle in the marketplace, and said to them, 'You also go into the vineyard, and whatever is right I will give you.' So they went. Again, he went out about the sixth and the ninth hour, and did likewise. And about the eleventh hour he went out and found others standing idle, and said to them, 'Why have you been standing here idle all day?' They said to him, 'Because no one hired us.' He said to them, 'You also go into the vineyard, and whatever is right you will receive.'

"When evening had come, the owner of the vineyard said to his manager, 'Call the labourers and give them their wages, beginning with the last to the first.' And when those came who were hired about the eleventh hour, they each received a denarius. But when the first came, they supposed that they would receive more; and they all received each a denarius. And when they had received it, they complained against the landowner, saying, 'These last men have worked only one hour, and you made them equal to us who have worked and laboured in the heat of the day.' But he answered one of them and said, 'Friend, I am doing you no wrong. Did you not agree with me for a denarius? Take what is yours and go your way. I wish to give to this last man the same as to you. Is it not lawful for me to do what I wish with my own things? Or is your eye evil because I am good?'

So, the last will be first, and the first last. For many are called, but few chosen."

John 10:22-42

The Shepherd Knows His Sheep

Now it was the Feast of Dedication in Jerusalem, and it was winter. And Jesus walked in the temple, in Solomon's porch.

Then the Jews surrounded Him and said to Him, "How long do You keep us in doubt? If You are the Christ, tell us plainly."

Jesus answered them, "I told you, and you do not believe. The works that I do in My Father's name, they give evidence and witness of Me. But you do not believe, because you are not of My sheep, as I said to you. My sheep hear My voice, and I know them, and they follow Me. And I give them eternal life, and they shall never perish; neither shall anyone snatch them out of My hand. My Father, who has given them to Me, is greater than all; and no one is able to snatch them out of My Father's hand. I and My Father are one."

Renewed Efforts to Stone Jesus

Then the Jews took up stones again to stone Him.

Jesus said to them, "Many good works I have shown you from My Father. For which of those works do you stone Me?"

The Jews answered Him, saying, "For a good work we do not stone You, but for blasphemy, and because You, being a Man, make Yourself God."

Jesus replied, "Is it not written in your law, *'I said, "You are gods"'*? If He called them gods, to whom the word of God came (and the Scripture cannot be broken), do you say of Him whom the Father sanctified and sent into the world, 'You are blaspheming,' because I said, 'I am the Son of God'? If I do not do the works of My Father, do not believe Me; but if I do, though you do not believe Me, believe the works, that you may know and believe that the Father is in Me, and I in Him."

Then they sought again to seize Him, but He escaped out of their hand.

The Believers Beyond Jordan

And Jesus went away again beyond the Jordan to the place where John was baptizing at first, and there He stayed.

Then many came to Him and said, "John performed no sign, but all the things that John spoke about this Man were true."

And many believed in Him there.

John 11:1-57

The Death of Lazarus

Now a certain man was sick, Lazarus of Bethany, the town of Mary and her sister Martha. It was that Mary who anointed the Lord with fragrant oil and wiped His feet with her hair, whose brother Lazarus was sick. Therefore, the sisters sent to Him, saying, "Lord, he whom You love is sick."

When Jesus heard that, He said, "This sickness is not unto death, but for the glory of God, that the Son of God may be glorified through it."

Now Jesus loved Martha and her sister and Lazarus. So, when He heard that Lazarus was sick, He stayed two more days in the place where He was. Then after this He said to the disciples, "Let us go to Judea again."

The disciples said to Him, "Rabbi, lately the Jews sought to stone You, and You are going there again?"

Jesus answered, "Are there not twelve hours in the day? If anyone walks in the day, he does not stumble, because he sees the light of this world. But if one walks in the night, he stumbles, because the light is not in him."

After that He said to them, "Our friend Lazarus sleeps, but I go that I may wake him up."

Then His disciples said, "Lord, if he sleeps he will get well."

However, Jesus spoke of his death, but they thought that He was speaking about taking rest in sleep.

Then Jesus said to them plainly, "Lazarus is dead. And I am glad for your sakes that I was not there, that you may believe."

And Jesus said, "Let us go to him."

Then Thomas, who is called the Twin, said to his fellow disciples, "Let us also go, that we may die with Him."

I Am the Resurrection and the Life

When Jesus came, He found that he had already been in the tomb four days.

Now Bethany was near Jerusalem, about two miles away. And many of the Jews had joined the women around Martha and Mary, to comfort them concerning their brother.

Then Martha, as soon as she heard that Jesus was coming, went and met Him, but Mary was sitting in the house.

Now Martha said to Jesus, "Lord, if You had been here, my brother would not have died. But even now I know that whatever You ask of God, God will give You."

Jesus said to her, "Your brother will rise again."

Martha said to Him, "I know that he will rise again in the resurrection at the last day."

Jesus said to her, "I am the resurrection and the life. He who believes in Me, though he may die, he shall live. And whoever lives and believes in Me shall never die. Do you believe this?"

She said to Him, "Yes, Lord, I believe that You are the Christ, the Son of God, who is to come into the world."

Jesus and Death, the Last Enemy

And when Martha had said these things, she went her way and secretly called Mary her sister, saying, "The Teacher has come and is calling for you." As soon as Mary heard that, she got up quickly and came to Him.

Now Jesus had not yet come into the town, but was in the place where Martha met Him.

Then the Jews who were with Mary in the house, and comforting her, when they saw that she got up quickly and went out, followed her, saying, "She is going to the tomb to weep there."

Then, when Mary came where Jesus was, and saw Him, she fell down at His feet, saying to Him, "Lord, if You had been here, my brother would not have died."

For this reason, when Jesus saw her weeping, and the Jews who came with her weeping, He groaned in the spirit and was troubled.

And Jesus said, "Where have you laid him?"

They said to Him, "Lord, come and see."

Jesus wept.

Then the Jews said, "See how He loved him!"

And some of them said, "Could not this Man, who opened the eyes of the blind, also have kept this man from dying?"

Lazarus Raised from the Dead

Then Jesus, again groaning in Himself, came to the tomb. It was a cave, and a stone lay against it.

Jesus said, "Take away the stone."

Martha, the sister of him who was dead, said to Him, "Lord, by this time there is a stench, for he has been dead four days."

Jesus said to her, "Did I not say to you that if you would believe you would see the glory of God?"

Then they took away the stone from the place where the dead man was lying.

And Jesus lifted up His eyes and said, "Father, I thank You that You have heard Me. And I know that You always hear Me, but because of the people who are standing by I said this, that they may believe that You sent Me."

Now when He had said these things, He cried with a loud voice, "Lazarus, come out!"

And he who had died came out bound hand and foot with grave clothes, and his face was wrapped with a cloth.

Jesus said to them, "Loose him, and let him go."

The Plot to Kill Jesus

Then many of the Jews who came to Mary, and had seen the things Jesus did, believed in Him. But some of them went away to the Pharisees and told them the things Jesus did.

Then the chief priests and the Pharisees gathered a council and said, "What shall we do? For this Man works many signs. If we let Him alone like this, everyone will believe in Him, and the Romans will come and take away both our place and nation."

And one of them, Caiaphas, being high priest that year, said to them, "You know nothing at all, or do you consider that it is necessary for us that one man should die for the people, and not that the whole nation should perish."

Now this he did not say on his own authority; but being high priest that year he prophesied that Jesus would die for the nation, and not for that nation only, but also that He would gather together in one the children of God who were scattered abroad.

Then, from that day on, they plotted to put Him to death. Jesus no longer walked openly among the Jews, but went from there into the country near the wilderness, to a city called Ephraim, and there remained with His disciples.

And the Passover of the Jews was near, and many went from the country up to Jerusalem before the Passover, to purify themselves. Then they sought Jesus, and spoke among themselves as they stood in the temple, "What do you think, that He will not come to the feast?"

Now both the chief priests and the Pharisees had given a command, that if anyone knew where He was, he should report it, that they might seize Him.

Matthew 20:17-28, Mark 10:32-45, Luke 18:31-34

Jesus a Third Time Predicts His Death and Resurrection

Now Jesus and His disciples were on the road, going up to Jerusalem, and Jesus was going before them; and they were amazed. And as they followed they were afraid. Then He took the twelve aside again and began to tell them the things that would happen to Him.

Jesus said to them, "We are going up to Jerusalem, and all things that are written by the prophets concerning the Son of Man will be accomplished. The Son of Man will be betrayed to the chief priests and to the scribes; and they will condemn Him to death and deliver Him to the Gentiles; and they will mock Him, and scourge

Him, and spit on Him, and kill, crucify Him. And the third day He will rise again."

But they understood none of these things. This saying was hidden from them, and they did not know the things which were spoken.

Greatness Is Serving

Then the mother of Zebedee's sons came to Jesus with her sons, James and John, kneeling down and asking something from Him.

And He said to her, "What do you wish?"

She said to Him, "Grant that these two sons of mine may sit, one on Your right hand and the other on the left, in Your kingdom."

But Jesus answered and said, "You do not know what you ask?" And turning to James and John He said, "Are you able to drink the cup that I drink, and be baptized with the baptism that I am baptized with?"

They said to Him, "We are able."

Jesus said to them, "You will indeed drink the cup that I drink, and with the baptism I am baptized with you will be baptized; but to sit on My right hand and on My left is not Mine to give, but it is for those for whom it is prepared."

And when the other ten disciples heard it, they began to be greatly displeased with James and John.

But Jesus called them all to Himself and said to them, "You know that those who are considered rulers over the Gentiles lord it over them, and their great ones exercise authority over them. Yet it shall not be so among you; but whoever desires to become great among you shall be your servant. And whoever of you desires to be first shall be slave of all. For even the Son of Man did not come to be served, but to serve, and to give His life a ransom for many."

Mark 10:46-52, Luke 18:35-43

Jesus Heals Blind Bartimaeus

Now Jesus came near to Jericho with His disciples and a great multitude followed.

Now a certain blind man, Bartimaeus, the son of Timaeus, sat by the road begging. And hearing a multitude passing by, he asked what it meant. They told him that Jesus of Nazareth was passing by. And when he heard that it was Jesus of Nazareth, he began to cry out and say, "Jesus, Son of David, have mercy on me!"

Then those who went before warned him that he should be quiet; but he cried out all the more, "Son of David, have mercy on me!"

Jesus stood still and commanded him to be brought to Him.

Then they called the blind man, saying to him, "Be of good cheer. Get up, He is calling you." And throwing aside his garment, he stood up and made his way to Jesus.

And when he had come near, Jesus asked him, saying, "What do you want Me to do for you?"

The blind man said to Him, "Rabboni, Lord, that I may receive my sight."

Then Jesus said to him, "Receive your sight. Go your way; your faith has made you well."

And immediately he received his sight, and followed Him on the road, glorifying God. And all the people, when they saw what had happened, gave praise to God as well.

Luke 19:1-27

Jesus Comes to Zacchaeus' House

Now Jesus entered and was passing through Jericho.

There was a man named Zacchaeus who was a chief tax collector, and he was rich. And he sought to see who Jesus was, but could not because of the crowd, for he was of short stature. Zacchaeus ran ahead and climbed up into a sycamore tree to see Him, for He was going to pass that way.

And when Jesus came to the place, He looked up and saw him, and said to him, "Zacchaeus, make haste and come down, for today I must stay at your house."

He made haste and came down, and received Him joyfully.

But when the Pharisees saw it, they all complained, saying, "He has gone to be a guest with a man who is a sinner."

Then Zacchaeus stood and said to the Lord, "Look, Lord, I give half of my goods to the poor; and if I have taken anything from anyone by false accusation, I restore him four time the amount."

And Jesus said to him, "Today salvation has come to this house, because he also is a son of Abraham; for the Son of Man has come to seek and to save that which was lost."

The Parable of the Minas

Now as they heard these things, Jesus spoke another parable, because He was near Jerusalem and they thought the kingdom of God would appear immediately.

Jesus said: "A certain nobleman went into a far country to receive for himself a kingdom and to return. He called ten of his servants, delivered to them ten minas, and said to them, 'Do business till I come.' But his citizens hated him, and sent a delegation after him, saying, 'We will not have this man to rule over us.'

"And so, it was that when he returned, having received the kingdom, he then commanded these servants, to whom he had given the money, to be called to him, that he might know how much every man had gained by trading. Then came the first, saying, 'Master, your mina has earned ten minas.' And he said to him, 'Well done, good servant; because you were faithful in a very little, have authority over ten cities.' And the second came, saying, 'Master, your mina has earned five minas.' Likewise, he said to him, 'You also be over five cities.' Then another came, saying, 'Master, here is your mina, which I have kept safely in a handkerchief. For I feared you, because you are a severe and strict man. You collect what you did not deposit, and reap what you did not sow.'

And he said to him, 'Out of your own mouth I will judge you, you wicked servant. You knew that I was a severe and strict man, collecting what I did not deposit and reaping what I did not sow. Why then did you not put my money in the bank, that at my coming I might have collected it with interest?'

"And he said to those who stood by, 'Take the mina from him, and give it to him who has ten minas.' (But they said to him, 'Master, he has ten minas.') 'For I say to you, that to everyone who has will be given; and from him who does not have, even what he has will be taken away from him. But bring here those enemies of mine, who did not want me to reign over them, and slay them before me.'"

Matthew 20:29-34

Two Blind Men Receive Their Sight

Now as Jesus and the disciples went out of Jericho, a great multitude followed Him.

And, two blind men sitting by the road, when they heard that Jesus was passing by, cried out, saying, "Have mercy on us, O Lord, Son of David!"

Then the multitude warned them that they should be quiet; but they cried out all the more, saying, "Have mercy on us, O Lord, Son of David!"

Jesus stood still and called them, and said, "What do you want Me to do for you?"

They said to Him, "Lord, that our eyes may be opened."

Jesus had compassion and touched their eyes. And immediately their eyes received sight, and they followed Him.

John 12:1-11

The Anointing at Bethany

Then, six days before the Passover, Jesus came to Bethany, where Lazarus was who had been dead, and had raised from the dead to life. There they made Him a supper; and Martha served, but Lazarus was one of those who sat at the table with Him. Then Mary took a pound of very costly oil of spikenard, anointed the feet of Jesus, and wiped His feet with her hair. And the house was filled with the fragrance of the oil.

But one of His disciples, Judas Iscariot, Simon's son, who would betray Him, said, "Why was this fragrant oil not sold for three hundred denarii and given to the poor?" This he said, not that he cared for the poor, but because he was a thief, and had the money box; and he used to take what was put in it.

But Jesus said, "Let her alone; she has kept this for the day of My burial. For the poor you have with you always, but Me you do not have always."

The Plot to Kill Lazarus

Now a great many of the Jews knew that He was there; and they came, not for Jesus' sake only, but that they might also see Lazarus, whom He had raised from the dead. But the chief priests plotted to put Lazarus to death also, because on account of him many of the Jews went away and believed in Jesus.

Matthew 21:1-11, Mark 11:1-11, Luke 19:28-44, John 12:12-19

The Triumphal Entry

The next day, a great multitude that had come for the feast of the Passover, heard that Jesus was coming to Jerusalem. Jesus went on ahead of the disciple and His followers.

As Jesus drew near to Jerusalem, near Bethphage and Bethany, at the mountain called Olivet or the Mount of Olives, He sent two of His disciples, saying, "Go into the village opposite you, where, as you enter you will find a donkey tied, and a colt with her, the foal of a donkey, on which no one has ever sat. Loose them and bring them here to Me. And if anyone asks you, "What are you doing? 'Why are you untying them?', you shall say to them, 'Because the Lord has need of them,' and immediately he will send them here."

All this was done that it might be fulfilled which was spoken by the prophet, saying:

"Tell the daughter of Zion,
'Behold, your King is coming to you,
Lowly, and sitting on a donkey,
A colt, the foal of a donkey.'"

So those who were sent, went their way and found the donkey and the colt tied by the door outside on the street, just as He had said to them. But as they were untying the colt, the owners and some of those who stood there said to them, "Why are you untying the colt?" And they spoke to them just as Jesus had commanded.

And the two disciples said, "The Lord has need of them." So, they let them go.

The disciples brought the donkey and the colt to Jesus, and laid their own clothes on them, and set Jesus on them. And as He went, many spread their clothes on the road.

As Jesus was now close to the descent of the Mount of Olives, the whole multitude of the disciples began to rejoice and praise God with a loud voice for all the mighty works they had seen, saying:

"Blessed is the King who comes in the name of the Lord!
The King of Israel!
Blessed is the kingdom of our father David
That comes in the name of the Lord! Hosanna.
Peace in heaven and glory in the highest!"

And many spread their clothes on the road, and others cut down leafy branches from the trees and took branches of palm trees and spread them on the road, and went out to meet Him. Then those who went before and those who followed cried out, saying:

"Hosanna! Blessed is He who comes in the name of the Lord!"

In this way, Jesus fulfilled the prophesy, for it is written:

"Fear not, daughter of Zion.
Behold, your King is coming,
Sitting on a donkey's colt."

His disciples did not understand these things at first, but when Jesus was glorified, then they remembered that these things were written about Him and that they had done these things to Him.

Now the people who were with Him when He called Lazarus out of his tomb and raised him from the dead, bore witness. For this reason, the people also met Him, because they heard that He had done this sign.

The Pharisees said among themselves, "You see that we are accomplishing nothing. Look, the world has gone after Him!" And some of the Pharisees called to Him from the crowd, "Teacher, rebuke Your disciples."

But He answered and said to them, "I tell you that if these should keep silent, the stones would immediately cry out."

And when He had come into Jerusalem, all the city was moved, saying, "Who is this?" So, the multitudes said, "This is Jesus, the prophet from Nazareth of Galilee."

And Jesus went into Jerusalem and into the temple.

When He had looked around at all things, as the hour was already late, He went out to Bethany with the twelve.

Jesus Weeps over Jerusalem

Now as He drew near, Jesus saw the city and wept over it, saying, "If you had known, even you, especially in this your day, the things that make for your peace! But now they are hidden from your eyes. For days will come upon you when your enemies will build an embankment around you, surround you and close you in on every side, and level you, and your children within you, to the ground; and they will not leave in you one stone upon another, because you did not know the time of your visitation."

Matthew 21:12-17, Mark 11:15-19, Luke 19:45-48

Jesus Cleanses the Temple

Jesus and His disciples came to Jerusalem, where Jesus went into the temple of God and began to drive out those who bought and sold in the temple, and overturned the tables of the money changers and the seats of those who sold doves. And He would not allow anyone to carry wares through the temple.

And He said to them, "Is it not written, *'My house shall be called a house of prayer for all nations'*? But you have made it a *'den of thieves.'"*

Then the blind and the lame came to Him in the temple, and He healed them.

But when the chief priests and scribes saw the wonderful things that He did, and the children crying out in the temple and saying, "Hosanna to the Son of David!" they were annoyed and angry and said to Him, "Do You hear what these are saying?"

And Jesus said to them, "Yes. Have you never read:

*'Out of the mouth of babes and nursing infants
You have perfected praise'*?"

And He was teaching daily in the temple. But the chief priests, the scribes, and the leaders of the people, when they heard it, sought how they might destroy Him, and were unable to do anything; for all the people were very attentive to hear Him. The chief priests, the scribes, and the leaders of the people feared Him, because all the people were astonished at His teaching.

When evening had come, He left them and went out of the city to Bethany, and He lodged there.

Matthew 21:18-22, Mark 11:12-14, 20-26

The Fig Tree Withered

Now the next day, when the disciples and Jesus came out from Bethany, returning to the city, He was hungry. And seeing from a distance, a fig tree by the road, having leaves, He went to see if perhaps He would find something on it. When He came to it, He found nothing but leaves, for it was not the season for figs.

Jesus said to it, "Let no fruit grow on you ever again," and His disciples heard it. Immediately the fig tree withered away.

The Lesson of the Withered Fig Tree

Now, as Jesus and His followers passed by, when the disciples saw the fig tree dried up from the roots they marvelled, saying, "How did the fig tree wither away so soon?"

And Peter, remembering, said to Him, "Rabbi, look! The fig tree which You cursed has withered away."

Jesus answered and said to them, "Have faith in God. I say to you, whoever says to this mountain, 'Be removed and be cast into the sea,' and does not doubt in his heart, but believes that those things he says will be done, he will have whatever he says. Therefore, I say to you, whatever things you ask when you pray, believe that you receive them, and you will have them.

Forgiveness and Prayer

"And whenever you stand praying, if you have anything against anyone, forgive him, that your Father in heaven may also forgive you your offences. But if you do not forgive, neither will your Father in heaven forgive your offences."

Matthew 21:23-32, Mark 11:27-33, Luke 20:1-8

Jesus' Authority Questioned

Then Jesus and the disciples came again to Jerusalem.

Now when He came walking into the temple, Jesus taught the people in the temple and preached the gospel.

The chief priests and the elders of the people confronted Him as He was teaching, and said, "By what authority are You doing these things? And who gave You this authority to do these things?"

But Jesus answered and said to them, "I also will ask you one question; then answer Me, and I will tell you by what authority I do these things. The baptism of John, was it from heaven or from men? Answer Me."

And they talked among themselves, saying, "If we say, 'From heaven,' He will say, 'Why then did you not believe him?' But if we say, 'From men,' they feared the people, for all counted John to have been a prophet. They answered and said to Jesus, 'We do not know.'"

And Jesus answered and said to them, "Neither will I tell you by what authority I do these things."

The Parable of the Two Sons

Jesus continued. "What do you think? A man had two sons, and he came to the first and said, 'Son, go, work today in my vineyard.' He answered and said, 'I will not,' but afterward he regretted it and went. Then he came to the second and said likewise. And he answered and said, 'I will go sir,' but he did not go. Which of the two did the will of his father?"

They said to Him, "The first."

Jesus said to them, "I say to you that tax collectors and harlots enter the kingdom of God before you. For John came to you in the way of righteousness, and you did not believe him; but tax collectors and harlots believed him; and when you saw it, you did not afterward relent and believe him."

Matthew 21:33 to 22:14, Mark 12:1-12, Luke 20:9-19

The Parable of the Wicked Vinedressers

Then Jesus began to speak to them in parables: "There was a certain landowner who planted a vineyard and set a hedge around it, dug a place for a winepress and vat in it, and built a tower. And he leased it to vinedressers and went into a far country for a long time. Now when vintage-time drew near, he sent his servants to the vinedressers, that they might receive some of the fruit of the vineyard from the vinedressers. And the vinedressers took his servants, killed one, stoned one, and beat another, and sent him away empty-handed. Again, he sent other servants, more than the first, and they did likewise to them. They threw stones, wounded one in the head, and sent him away shamefully treated. And again, he sent a third; and they wounded him also and threw him out. Then last of all still having one son, his beloved, he also sent him to them, saying, 'They will respect my son.' But when the vinedressers saw the son, they said among themselves, 'This is the heir. Come, let us kill him and seize his inheritance. So, they took him and cast him out of the vineyard and killed him. Therefore, when the owner of the vineyard comes, what will he do to those vinedressers?"

Then Jesus said to them, "He will destroy those wicked men miserably, and lease his vineyard to other vinedressers who will render to him the fruits in their seasons."

And when they heard it they said, "Certainly not!"

Then Jesus looked at them and said, "Have you never read in the Scriptures:

'The stone which the builders rejected
Has become the chief cornerstone.
This was the Lord's doing,
And it is marvellous in our eyes'?

"Therefore, I say to you, the kingdom of God will be taken from you and given to a nation bearing the fruits of it. And whoever falls on this stone will be broken; but on whomever it falls, it will grind him to powder."

Now when the chief priests and Pharisees heard His parables, they understood that He was speaking about them. And the chief priests and the scribes that very hour sought to lay hands on Jesus, but they feared the multitudes, for they knew He had spoken the parable against them, because they took Him for a prophet. So, they left Him and went away.

The Parable of the Wedding Feast

After Jesus had answered, He spoke to those in the temple by parables saying: "The kingdom of heaven is like a certain king who arranged a marriage for his son, and sent out his servants to call those who were invited to the wedding; and they were not willing to come. Again, he sent out other servants, saying, 'Tell those who are invited, "See, I have prepared my dinner; my oxen and fatted cattle are killed, and all things are ready. Come to the wedding."' But the invited guests made light of it and went their ways, one to his own farm, another to his business. And the rest seized his servants, treated them cruelly, and killed them. But when the king heard about it, he was furious. And he sent out his armies, destroyed those murderers, and burned up their city. Then he said to his servants, 'The wedding is ready, but those who were invited were not worthy. Now I say to you, go into the highways, and as many as you find, invite to the wedding.' So those servants went out into the highways and gathered together all whom they found, both bad and good. And the wedding hall was filled with guests.

"But when the king came in to see the guests, he saw a man there who did not have on a wedding garment. He said to him, 'Friend, how did you come in here without a wedding garment?' And he was speechless. Then the king said to the servants, 'Bind him hand and foot, take him away, and throw him into outer darkness; there will be weeping and gnashing of teeth.'

"For many are called, but few are chosen."

Matthew 22:15-22, Mark 12:13-17, Luke 20:20-26

The Pharisees: Is It Lawful to Pay Taxes to Caesar?

Then the Pharisees went and plotted how they might entangle Jesus in His talk. So, they watched Him, and sent spies who pretended to be righteous, some of the Pharisees and the Herodians, to catch Him in His words, in order to deliver Him to the power and the authority of the governor.

When they came, they asked Him, "Teacher, we know that You say and teach rightly, and You do not show personal favouritism, for You do not regard the person of men but teach the way of God in truth. Tell us, what You think? Is it lawful to pay taxes to Caesar, or not? Shall we pay, or shall we not pay?"

But Jesus knowing their wickedness, hypocrisy and craftiness said, "Why do you test Me, you hypocrites? Show Me the tax money." So, they brought Him a denarius.

And He said to them, "Whose image and inscription is this?"

They said to Him, "Caesar's."

And Jesus answered and said to them, "Render to Caesar the things that are Caesar's, and to God the things that are God's."

When they had heard these words, they marvelled, but they could not catch Him in His words and at His answer and kept silent in the presence of the people. Then they left Him and went their way.

Matthew 22:23-33, Mark 12:18-27, Luke 20:27-40

The Sadducees: What About the Resurrection?

The same day the Sadducees, who deny and say there is no resurrection, came to Jesus and asked Him saying, "Teacher, Moses wrote for us that if a man's brother dies, and leaves his wife behind, and leaves no children, his brother should take his wife and raise up the offspring for his brother. Now there were seven brothers. And the first took a wife, and died without children. And the second took her as wife, and he died childless. Then the third took her, and in like manner the seven also; and they left no children, all the seven died. Last of all the woman died. In the resurrection, when they rise, whose wife will she become? For all seven had her as wife."

Jesus answered and said to them, "You are mistaken, because you do not know the Scriptures or the power of God. For in the resurrection when they rise from the dead, they neither marry or are given in marriage, but are like angels of God in heaven.

"But concerning the resurrection of the dead, have you not read in the book of Moses, in the burning bush passage, what was spoken to you by God, saying, *'I am the God of Abraham, the God of Isaac, and the God of Jacob'*? God is not the God of the dead, but of the living, for all live to Him. You are greatly mistaken."

Jesus said to them, "The sons of this age marry and are given in marriage. But those who are counted worthy to attain that age, and the resurrection from the dead, neither marry or are given in marriage; or can they die anymore, for they are equal to the angels and are sons of God, being sons of the resurrection."

And when the multitudes heard this, they were astonished at His teaching.

Then some of the scribes answered and said, "Teacher, You have spoken well." But after that they dared not question Him anymore.

Matthew 22:34-46, Mark 12:28-37, Luke 20:41-44

The Scribes: Which Is the First Commandment of All?

But when the Pharisees heard that Jesus had silenced the Sadducees, they gathered together.

Then one of the scribes came, and having heard them reasoning together, understanding that He had answered them well, asked Him a question, testing Him, and saying, "Teacher, which is the great commandment in the law?"

Jesus answered him, "The first of all the commandments is: *'Hear, O Israel, the Lord our God, the Lord is one. And you shall love the Lord your God with all your heart, with all your soul, with all your mind, and with all your strength.'* This is the first commandment.

And the second, like it, is this: *'You shall love your neighbour as yourself.'* There is no other commandment greater than these. On these two commandments hang all the Law and the Prophets."

The scribe said to Him, "Well said, Teacher. You have spoken the truth, for there is one God, and there is no other but He. And to love Him with all the heart, with all the understanding, with all the soul, and with all the strength, and to love one's neighbour as oneself, is more than all the whole burnt offerings and sacrifices."

Now when Jesus saw that he answered wisely, He said to him, "You are not far from the kingdom of God."

But after that no one dared question Him.

Jesus: How Can David Call His Descendant Lord?

While the Pharisees were gathered together, as Jesus taught in the temple, He asked them, saying, "What do you think about the Christ? Whose Son is He?"

They said to Him, "The Son of David."

And He said to them, "How can you say that the Christ is the Son of David? For David himself, by the Holy Spirit, in the Book of Psalms, called Him 'Lord,' saying:

'The Lord said to my Lord,
"Sit at My right hand,
Till I make Your enemies Your footstool."'

If David then calls Him 'Lord,' how is He his Son?"

And no one was able to answer Him a word, nor from that day on did anyone dare question Him anymore. And the common people heard Him gladly.

Matthew 23:1-39, Mark 12:38-44, Luke 20:45 to 21:4

Woe to the Scribes and Pharisees

Then Jesus spoke to the multitudes and to His disciples, saying: "The scribes and the Pharisees sit in Moses' seat. Therefore, whatever they tell you to observe, that observe and do, but do not do according to their works; for they say, and do not do. For they bind heavy burdens, hard to bear, and lay them on men's shoulders; but they themselves will not move them with one of their fingers. But all their works they do to be seen by men. They make their phylacteries broad and enlarge the borders of their garments. They love the best places at feasts, the best seats in the synagogues, greetings in the marketplaces, and to be called by men, 'Rabbi, Rabbi.' But you, do not be called 'Rabbi'; for One is your Teacher, the Christ, and you are all brethren. Do not call anyone on earth your father; for One is your Father, He who is in heaven. And do not be called teachers; for One is your Teacher, the Christ. But he who is greatest among you shall be your servant. And whoever exalts himself will be humbled, and he who humbles himself will be exalted.

"But woe to you, scribes and Pharisees, hypocrites! For you shut up the kingdom of heaven against men; for you neither go in yourselves, or do you allow those who are entering to go in.

"Woe to you, scribes and Pharisees, hypocrites! For you devour widows' houses, and for a pretence make long prayers. Therefore, you will receive greater condemnation.

"Woe to you, scribes and Pharisees, hypocrites! For you travel land and sea to win one proselyte, and when he is won, you make him twice as much a son of hell as yourselves.

"Woe to you, blind guides, who say, 'Whoever swears by the temple, it is nothing; but whoever swears by the gold of the temple, he is obliged to perform it.' Fools and blind! For which is greater, the gold or the temple that sanctifies the gold? And, 'Whoever swears by the altar, it is nothing; but whoever swears by the gift that is on it, he is obliged to perform it.' Fools and blind! For which is greater, the gift or the altar that sanctifies the gift? Therefore, he who swears by the altar, swears by it and by all things on it. He who swears by the temple, swears by it and by Him who dwells in it. And he who swears by heaven, swears by the throne of God and by Him who sits on it.

"Woe to you, scribes and Pharisees, hypocrites! For you pay tithe of mint and anise and cumin, and have neglected the weightier matters of the law: justice and mercy and faith. These you should have done, without leaving the others undone. Blind guides, who strain out a gnat and swallow a camel!

"Woe to you, scribes and Pharisees, hypocrites! For you cleanse the outside of the cup and dish, but inside they are full of extortion and self-indulgence. Blind Pharisee, first cleanse the inside of the cup and dish, that the outside of them may be clean also.

"Woe to you, scribes and Pharisees, hypocrites! For you are like whitewashed tombs which indeed appear beautiful outwardly, but inside are full of dead men's bones and all uncleanness. Even so, you also outwardly appear righteous to men, but inside you are full of hypocrisy and lawlessness.

"Woe to you, scribes and Pharisees, hypocrites! Because you build the tombs of the prophets and adorn the monuments of the righteous, and say, 'If we had lived in the days of our fathers, we would not have been partakers with them in the blood of the prophets.'

"For this reason, you are witnesses against yourselves that you are sons of those who murdered the prophets. Fill up, then, the measure of your fathers' guilt. Serpents, brood of vipers! How can you escape the condemnation of hell?

"For this reason, I send you prophets, wise men, and scribes: some of them you will kill and crucify, and some of them you will scourge in your synagogues and persecute from city to city, that on you may come all the righteous blood shed on the earth, from the blood of righteous Abel to the blood of Zechariah, son of Berechiah, whom you murdered between the temple and the altar. I say to you; all these things will come upon this generation.

Jesus Laments over Jerusalem

"O Jerusalem, Jerusalem, the one who kills the prophets and stones those who are sent to her! How often I wanted to gather your children together, as a hen gathers her chicks under her wings, but you were not willing! See! Your house is left to you desolate; for I say to you, you shall see Me no more till you say, *'Blessed is He who comes in the name of the Lord!'*"

Beware of the Scribes

Then, in the hearing of all the people, Jesus said to His disciples, "Beware of the scribes, who desire to go around in long robes, love greetings in the marketplaces, the best seats in the synagogues, and the best places at feasts, who devour widows' houses, and for a pretence make long prayers. These will receive greater condemnation."

The Widow's Two Mites

Now Jesus sat opposite the treasury. And He looked up and saw the rich putting their gifts into the treasury, and saw how the people put money into the treasury. And many who were rich put in much. Then one poor widow came and threw in two mites, which make a quadrans.

So, He called His disciples to Himself and said to them, "Truly, I say to you that this poor widow has put in more than all those who have given to the treasury; for they all put in, out of their abundance, their offerings for God. But she out of her poverty put in all that she had, her whole livelihood."

Matthew 24:1-35, Mark 13:1-31, Luke 21:5-33

Jesus Predicts the Destruction of the Temple

Then Jesus went out and departed from the temple. As He went out of the temple, His disciples came up to show Him the buildings of the temple.

One of His disciples said to Him, "Teacher, see what manner of stones and what buildings are here!"

Then, as some spoke of the temple, how it was adorned with beautiful stones and donations, Jesus answered and said to him, "Do you see all these great buildings? Truly, the day will come when not one stone shall be left upon another, that shall not be thrown down."

The Signs of the Times and the End of the Age

Now as Jesus sat on the Mount of Olives opposite the temple, Peter, James, John, and Andrew asked Him privately, "Teacher, when will these things be? And what will be the sign when all these things will be fulfilled? And what will be the sign of Your coming, and the end of the age?"

And Jesus, answering them, said, "Take note that no one deceives you. For many will come in My name, saying, 'I am He,'

'I am the Christ' and, 'The time has drawn near,' and will deceive many. But when you hear of wars and rumours of wars, see that you are not troubled; for such things must happen, but this is not the end. The gospel must first be preached to all the nations. For nation will fight against nation, and kingdom against kingdom. And there will be earthquakes in various places, and there will be famines and pestilences, and there will be fearful sights and great signs from heaven. All these are the beginnings of sorrows.

"But watch out for yourselves, for they will deliver you up to tribulation and kill you, and you will be beaten in the synagogues, and put into prisons. You will be hated by all nations for My name's sake. You will be brought before rulers and kings for My sake, but it will turn out for you as an occasion for testimony to them. But when they arrest you and deliver you up, do not worry beforehand, or premeditate what you will speak. But whatever is given you in that hour, speak that; for it is not you who speak, but the Holy Spirit. Settle it in your hearts not to meditate beforehand on what you will answer; for I will give you a mouth and wisdom which all your enemies, your opponents, will not be able to contradict or resist. And then many will be offended. Brother will betray brother to death, and a father his child; and children will rise up against parents and cause them to be put to death. And you will be hated by all for My name's sake. Then many false prophets will come and deceive many. Lawlessness will be everywhere, the love of many will grow cold. But he who endures to the end shall be saved. Not a hair of your head shall be lost. Let patience possess your souls. And this gospel of the kingdom will be preached in all the world as a witness to all the nations, and then the end will come. But he who endures to the end shall be saved.

The Great Tribulation

"Therefore, when you see the *'abomination of desolation,'* spoken of by Daniel the prophet, standing in the holy place (whoever reads, let him understand), then let those who are in Judea flee to the mountains. Let him who is on the housetop not go down to take anything out of his house. And let him who is in the field not go back to get his clothes. But woe to those who are pregnant and to those who are nursing babies in those days! And pray that your flight may not be in winter or on the Sabbath. For then there will be great tribulation, such as has not been since the beginning of the world until this time, no, or ever shall be. And unless those days were shortened, no flesh would be saved; but for the elect's sake those days will be shortened.

"Then if anyone says to you, 'Look, here is the Christ!' or 'There!' do not believe it. For false christs and false prophets will rise and show great signs and wonders to deceive, if possible, even the elect. See, I have told you beforehand. If they say to you, 'Look, He is in the desert!' do not go out; or 'Look, He is in the inner rooms!' do not believe it. For as the lightning comes from the east and flashes to the west, so also will the coming of the Son of Man be. For wherever the carcass is, there the eagles will be gathered together.

The Coming of the Son of Man

"Immediately after the tribulation of those days, there will be signs in the sun, in the moon, and in the stars; and on the earth distress of nations, lost understanding, the sea and the waves roaring; men's hearts failing them from fear and the expectation of those things which are coming on the earth, for the powers of the heavens will be shaken. The sun will be darkened, and the moon will not give its light; the stars will fall from heaven. Then the sign of the Son of

Man will appear in heaven, and then all the people of the earth will mourn, and they will see the Son of Man coming on the clouds of heaven with power and great glory. And He will send His angels with a great sound of a trumpet, and they will gather together His elect from the four winds, from one end of heaven to the other. Now when these things begin to happen, look up and lift up your heads, because your redemption draws near."

The Parable of the Fig Tree

Then Jesus spoke to them a parable saying, "Learn from the fig tree. 'Look at the fig tree, and all the trees. When its branch has already become tender and puts forth leaves, when they are already budding, you see and know that summer is near'. When you see these things happening, know that the kingdom of God is near, at the door! I say to you, this generation will by no means pass away till all these things take place. Heaven and earth will pass away, but My words will by no means pass away.

The Destruction of Jerusalem

"But when you see Jerusalem surrounded by armies, then know that its desolation is near. Then let those who are in Judea flee to the mountains, let those who are in the midst of her depart, and let not those who are in the country enter her. For these are the days of vengeance, that all things which are written may be fulfilled. But woe to those who are pregnant and to those who are nursing babies in those days! For there will be great distress in the land and extreme anger upon this people. And they will fall by the edge of the sword, and be led away captive into all nations. And Jerusalem will be trampled by Gentiles until the times of the Gentiles are fulfilled."

Matthew 24:36 to 25:46, Mark 13:32-37, Luke 21:34-38

No One Knows the Day or Hour

Then Jesus said, "But of that day and hour no one knows, not even the angels of heaven, or the Son, but My Father only. But as the days of Noah were, so also will the coming of the Son of Man be. For as in the days before the flood, they were eating and drinking, marrying and giving in marriage, until the day that Noah entered the ark, and did not know until the flood came and took them all away, so also will the coming of the Son of Man be. Take notice, watch and pray; for you do not know when the time is. It is like a man going to a far country, who left his house and gave authority to his servants, and to each his work, and commanded the doorkeeper to watch. Watch I say, for you do not know when the master of the house is coming. Maybe in the evening, at midnight, at the crowing of the rooster, or in the morning. Don't let His coming suddenly find you sleeping. Then two men will be in the field: one will be taken and the other left. Two women will be grinding at the mill: one will be taken and the other left. Watch, for you do not know what hour your Lord is coming. But know this, that if the master of the house had known what hour the thief would come, he would have watched and not allowed his house to be broken into. I say to you, be ready, for the Son of Man is coming at an hour you do not expect. And what I say to you, I say to all: Watch!

The Faithful Servant and the Evil Servant

"Who then is a faithful and wise servant, whom his master made ruler over his household, to give them food in due season? Blessed is that servant whom his master, when he comes, will find so doing.

I say to you that he will make him ruler over all his goods. But if that evil servant says in his heart, 'My master is delaying his coming,' and begins to beat his fellow servants, and to eat and drink with the drunkards, the master of that servant will come on a day when he is not looking for him and at an hour that he is not aware of, and will cut him in two and appoint him his portion with the hypocrites. There shall be weeping and gnashing of teeth.

The Parable of the Wise and Foolish Virgins

"Then the kingdom of heaven shall be likened to ten virgins who took their lamps and went out to meet the bridegroom. Now five of them were wise, and five were foolish. Those who were foolish took their lamps and took no oil with them, but the wise took oil in their vessels with their lamps. But while the bridegroom was delayed, they all slumbered and slept. And at midnight a cry was heard: 'Look, the bridegroom is coming; go out to meet him!' Then all those virgins woke and trimmed their lamps. And the foolish said to the wise, 'Give us some of your oil, for our lamps are going out.' But the wise answered, saying, 'No, in case there should not be enough for us and you; but go to those who sell, and buy for yourselves.' And while they went to buy, the bridegroom came, and those who were ready went in with him to the wedding; and the door was shut. Afterward the other virgins came also, saying, 'Lord, Lord, open to us!' But he answered and said, 'I say to you, I do not know you.' Watch therefore, for you know neither the day or the hour in which the Son of Man is coming.

The Parable of the Talents

"For the kingdom of heaven is like a man traveling to a far country, who called his own servants and delivered his goods to them. And to one he gave five talents, to another two, and to another one, to each according to his own ability; and immediately he went on a journey. Then he who had received the five talents went and traded with them, and made another five talents. And he who had received two gained two more. But he who had received one went and dug in the ground, and hid his lord's money. After a long time the lord of those servants came and settled accounts with them.

"So, he who had received five talents came and brought five other talents, saying, 'Lord, you gave me five talents; look, I have gained five more talents besides them.' His lord said to him, 'Well done, good and faithful servant; you were faithful over a few things, I will make you ruler over many things. Enter into the joy of your lord.' He also who had received two talents came and said, 'Lord, you gave me two talents; look, I have gained two more talents besides them.' His lord said to him, 'Well done, good and faithful servant; you have been faithful over a few things, I will make you ruler over many things. Enter into the joy of your lord.'

"Then he who had received the one talent came and said, 'Lord, I knew you to be a hard man, reaping where you have not sown, and gathering where you have not scattered seed. And I was afraid, and went and hid your talent in the ground. Look, there you have what is yours.'

"But his lord answered and said to him, 'You wicked and lazy servant, you knew that I reap where I have not sown, and gather where I have not scattered seed. You ought to have deposited my money with the bankers, and at my coming I would have received back my own with interest. Take the talent from him, and give it to him who has ten talents.

"For to everyone who has, more will be given, and he will have abundance; but from him who does not have, even what he has will be taken away. And throw the unprofitable servant into the outer darkness. There will be weeping and gnashing of teeth.

The Son of Man Will Judge the Nations

"When the Son of Man comes in His glory, and all the holy angels with Him, then He will sit on the throne of His glory. All the nations will be gathered before Him, and He will separate them one from another, as a shepherd divides his sheep from the goats. And He will set the sheep on His right hand, but the goats on the left. Then the King will say to those on His right hand, 'Come, you blessed of My Father, inherit the kingdom prepared for you from the foundation of the world: for I was hungry and you gave Me food; I was thirsty and you gave Me drink; I was a stranger and you took Me in; I was naked and you clothed Me; I was sick and you visited Me; I was in prison and you came to Me.'

"Then the righteous will answer Him, saying, 'Lord, when did we see You hungry and feed You, or thirsty and give You drink? When did we see You a stranger and take You in, or naked and clothe You? Or when did we see You sick, or in prison, and come to You?' And the King will answer and say to them, 'I say to you, considering you did this to one of the least of these My brothers, you did it to Me.' Then He will also say to those on the left hand, 'Depart from Me, you cursed, into the everlasting fire prepared for the devil and his angels: for I was hungry and you gave Me no food; I was thirsty and you gave Me no drink; I was a stranger and you did not take Me in, naked and you did not clothe Me, sick and in prison and you did not visit Me.'

"Then they also will answer Him, saying, 'Lord, when did we see You hungry or thirsty or a stranger or naked or sick or in prison, and did not minister to You?'

"Then He will answer them, saying, 'I say to you, considering you did not do it to one of the least of these, you did not do it to Me.' And these will go away into everlasting punishment, but the righteous into eternal life.

The Importance of Watching

"But take note to yourselves, don't let your hearts be weighed down with enjoying yourself noisily, drunkenness, and cares of this life, and that Day come on you unexpectedly. For it will come as a trap on all those who live on the face of the whole earth. Watch I say, and pray always that you may be counted worthy to escape all these things that will come to pass, and to stand before the Son of Man."

And in the daytime, He was teaching in the temple, but at night He went out and stayed on the mountain called Olivet. Then early in the morning all the people came to Him in the temple to hear Him.

John 12:20-50

The Fruitful Grain of Wheat

Now there were certain Greeks among those who came up to worship at the feast. They came to Philip, who was from Bethsaida of Galilee, and asked him, saying, "Sir, we wish to see Jesus."

Philip came and told Andrew, and in turn Andrew and Philip told Jesus.

But Jesus answered them, saying, "The hour has come that the Son of Man should be glorified. I say to you, unless a grain of wheat falls into the ground and dies, it remains alone; but if it dies, it produces much grain. He who loves his life will lose it, and he who hates his life in this world will keep it for eternal life. If anyone serves Me, let him follow Me; and where I am, there My servant will be also. If anyone serves Me, him My Father will honour.

Jesus Predicts His Death on the Cross

"Now My soul is troubled, and what shall I say? 'Father, save Me from this hour'? But for this purpose, I came to this hour. Father, glorify Your name."

Then a voice came from heaven, saying, "I have both glorified it and will glorify it again."

The people who stood by and heard it said that it had thundered. Others said, "An angel has spoken to Him."

Jesus answered and said, "This voice did not come because of Me, but for your sake. Now is the judgment of this world; now the ruler of this world will be cast out. And I, if I am lifted up from the earth, will draw all peoples to Myself." This He said, signifying by what death He would die.

The people answered Him, "We have heard from the law that the Christ remains forever; and how can You say, 'The Son of Man must be lifted up'? Who is this Son of Man?"

Then Jesus said to them, "A little while longer the light is with you. Walk while you have the light, unless darkness overtakes you; he who walks in darkness does not know where he is going. While you have the light, believe in the light, that you may become sons of light."

These things Jesus spoke, and departed, and was hidden from them.

Who Has Believed Our Report?

But although Jesus had done so many signs before them, they did not believe in Him, that the word of Isaiah the prophet might be fulfilled, which he spoke:

"Lord, who has believed our report?
And to whom has the arm of the Lord been revealed?"

This people could not believe, because Isaiah said again:

"He has blinded their eyes and hardened their hearts,
Lest they should see with their eyes,
Lest they should understand with their hearts and turn,
So that I should heal them."

These things Isaiah said when he saw His glory and spoke of Him.

Walk in the Light

In spite of that, even among the rulers many believed in Him, but because of the Pharisees they did not confess Him, for if they did, they should be put out of the synagogue; for they loved the praise of men more than the praise of God.

Then Jesus cried out and said, "He who believes in Me, believes not in Me but in Him who sent Me. And he who sees Me sees Him who sent Me. I have come as a light into the world, that whoever believes in Me should not be in darkness. And if anyone hears My words and does not believe, I do not judge him; for I did not come to judge the world but to save the world. He who rejects Me, and does not receive My words, has that which judges him, the word that I have spoken will judge him in the last day. For I have not spoken on My own authority; but the Father who sent Me gave Me a command, what I should say and what I should speak. And I know that His command is everlasting life. Listen to Me, whatever I speak, just as the Father has told Me, so I speak."

Matthew 26:1-16, Mark 14:1-11, Luke 22:1-6

The Plot to Kill Jesus

The Feast of Unleavened Bread was approaching, which is called Passover.

When Jesus had finished all these sayings, He said to His disciples, "You know that after two days is the Passover, and the Son of Man will be delivered up to be crucified."

Now the chief priests, the scribes, and the elders of the people assembled at the palace of the high priest, who was called Caiaphas, and plotted to take Jesus by trickery and put Him to death, kill Him. But they said, "Not during the feast, lest there be an uproar among the people." And the chief priests and the scribes sought how they might kill Him, for they feared the people.

Judas Agrees to Betray Jesus

Then Satan entered into Judas, surnamed Iscariot, who was numbered among the twelve. He went his way, met and talked with the chief priests and captains, how he might betray Jesus to them.

Judas said, "What are you willing to give me if I deliver Him to you?"

And they agreed to give him money. And they counted out to him thirty pieces of silver.

So, Judas promised and sought opportunity to betray Him to them in the absence of the multitude. And when the Pharisees heard it, they were glad. So, Judas sought how he might conveniently betray Him.

The Anointing at Bethany

And when Jesus was in Bethany at the house of Simon the leper, as He sat at the table, a woman came to Him having an alabaster flask of very costly fragrant oil of spikenard, and she poured it on His head.

But when His disciples saw it, they were angry and annoyed, saying, "Why this waste? For this fragrant oil might have been sold for much more than three hundred denarii and given to the poor." And they criticized her sharply.

But when Jesus was made aware of what had been said, He replied, "Let her alone. Why do you trouble the woman? For she has done a good work for Me. For you have the poor with you always, and whenever you wish you may do them good; but Me you do not have always. For in pouring this fragrant oil on My body, she came beforehand to anoint My body for burial. I tell you the truth, wherever this gospel is preached in the whole world, what this woman has done will also be told as a memorial to her."

Matthew 26:17-25, Mark 14:12-16, Luke 22:7-13

Jesus Celebrates Passover with His Disciples

Now on the first day of the Feast of the Unleavened Bread, when the Passover lamb was killed, the disciples came to Jesus and said to Him, "Where do You want us to go and prepare to eat the Passover?" And He chose Peter and John to make all things ready.

And Jesus said to them, "When you have entered the city, a man will meet you carrying a pitcher of water; follow him into the house which he enters. Then you shall say to the master of the house, 'The Teacher says to you, "My time is at hand; Where is the guest room in your house in which I will keep the Passover with

My disciples?"' Then he will show you a prepared large furnished upper room; there make ready."

So, His disciples went out, and came into the city, and found it just as He had said to them; and they prepared the Passover.

Luke 22:24-30

The Disciples Argue About Greatness

Now there was also a dispute among them, as to which of them should be considered the greatest.

And Jesus said to them, "The kings of the Gentiles exercise lordship over them, and those who exercise authority over them are called 'benefactors.' But not so among you; for we think opposite. He who is greatest among you, let him be as the younger, and he who governs as he who serves. For who is greater, he who sits at the table, or he who serves? Is it not he who sits at the table? Yet I am among you as the One who serves.

"But you are those who have continued with Me in My trials. And I present you with a kingdom, just as My Father presented one to Me, that you may eat and drink at My table in My kingdom, and sit on thrones judging the twelve tribes of Israel."

John 13:1-17

Jesus Washes the Disciples' Feet

Now before the Feast of the Passover, when Jesus knew His hour had come and He should depart from this world to the Father, having loved His own who were in the world, He loved them to the end.

During the meal, the devil having already put it into the heart of Judas Iscariot, Simon's son, to betray Him, Jesus, knowing that the Father had given all things into His hands, and that He had come from God and was going to God, rose from supper and took off some of His clothes, took a towel and tied it around His waist. After that, He poured water into a basin and began to wash the disciples' feet, and to wipe them with the towel with which He had wrapped around His waist.

Then He came to Simon Peter. And Peter said to Him, "Lord, are You washing my feet?"

Jesus answered and said to him, "What I am doing you do not understand now, but you will know after this."

Peter said to Him, "You shall never wash my feet!"

Jesus answered him, "If I do not wash you, you have no part with Me."

Simon Peter said to Him, "Lord, not my feet only, but also my hands and my head!"

Jesus replied, "He who has washed himself, needs only to wash his feet, and he is completely clean; and you are clean, but not all of you."

For He knew who would betray Him.

So, when He had washed their feet, taken His clothes, and sat down again, He said to them, "Do you know what I have done to you? You call Me Teacher and Lord, and you say well, for so I am. If I then, your Lord and Teacher, have washed your feet, you should also wash one another's feet. For I have given you an example, that you should do as I have done to you. I say to you; a servant is not greater than his master; nor is he who is sent greater than he who sent him. If you know these things, blessed are you if you do them."

Mark 14:17-21, John 13:18-30

Jesus Identifies His Betrayer

Now as they were eating, Jesus said, "I do not speak concerning all of you. I know whom I have chosen; but that the Scripture may be fulfilled, 'He who eats bread with Me has lifted up his heel against Me.' Now I tell you before it comes, that when it does come to pass, you may believe that I am He. I say to you, he who receives whomever I send receives Me; and he who receives Me receives Him who sent Me."

When Jesus had said these things, He was troubled in spirit, and testified and said, "I say to you, one of you will betray Me. The Son of Man goes just as it is written of Him, but woe to that man by whom the Son of Man is betrayed! It would have been good for that man if he had not been born."

Then the disciples looked at one another, puzzled about whom He spoke. And they began to be sorrowful, and to say to Him one by one, "Lord, is it I?" And another said, "Is it I?"

Now the disciple Jesus loved was leaning against Him. Simon Peter suggested that he ask Jesus who would betray him. Then, leaning back, he said to Him, "Lord, who is it?"

Jesus answered, "It is he to whom I shall give a piece of bread when I have dipped it."

And having dipped the bread, He gave it to Judas Iscariot, the son of Simon.

Then Judas, who was betraying Him, answered and said, "Rabbi, is it I?"

He said to him, "You have said it."

Now after Judas had received the piece of bread, Satan entered him.

Then Jesus said to him, "What you do, do quickly."

But no one at the table knew for what reason He said this to him. For some thought, because Judas had the money box, Jesus had said to him, "Buy those things we need for the feast," or that he should give something to the poor.

Having received the piece of bread, Judas went out immediately. And it was night.

John 13:31-35

The New Commandment

So, when Judas had gone out, Jesus said, "Now the Son of Man is glorified, and God is glorified in Him. If God is glorified in Him, God will also glorify Him in Himself, and glorify Him immediately. Little children, I shall be with you a little while longer. You will seek Me; and as I said to the Jews, 'Where I am going, you cannot come,' so now I say to you. A new commandment I give to you, that you love one another; as I have loved you, that you also love one another. By this all will know that you are My disciples, if you have love for one another."

Matthew 26:31-35, Mark 14:27-31, Luke 22:31-34, John 13:36-38

Jesus Predicts Peter's Denial

Simon Peter said to Him, "Lord, where are You going?"

Jesus answered him, "Where I am going you cannot follow Me now, but you shall follow Me afterward."

Peter said to Him, "Lord, why can I not follow You now? I will lay down my life for Your sake."

Jesus answered him, "Will you lay down your life for My sake?"

Then Jesus said to them, "All of you will be made to stumble because of Me this night, for it is written:

'I will strike the Shepherd,
And the sheep will be scattered.'

"But after I have been raised from the dead, I will go before you to Galilee."

Peter answered and said to Him, "Even if all are made to stumble because of You, I will never stumble."

And the Lord said, "Simon, Simon! Satan has asked for you, that he sift you as wheat. But I have prayed for you, that your faith should not fail; and when you have returned to Me, strengthen your brothers."

"Lord, I am ready to go with You, both to prison and to death," Peter replied.

Jesus said to him, "I say to you that today, even this night, before the rooster crows twice, you will deny Me three times."

But Peter spoke more forcefully and with passion, "If I have to die with You, I will not deny You!" And they all said likewise.

Matthew 26:26-30, Mark 14:22-25, Luke 22:14-23

Jesus Institutes the Lord's Supper

When the hour had come, Jesus said to them, "With fervent desire I have desired to eat this Passover with you before I suffer; for I say to you, I will no longer eat of it until it is fulfilled in the kingdom of God."

And as they were eating, Jesus took the bread, gave thanks and broke it, and gave it to the disciples and said, "This is My body which is given for you; do this in remembrance of Me."

Then He took the cup. And when He had given thanks, gave it to them, saying, "Take this and divide It among yourselves; Drink from it, all of you. For this is My blood of the new covenant, which is shed for many for the remission of sins. But I say to you, I will not drink of this fruit of the vine from now on until that day when I drink it new with you in My Father's kingdom."

Then, Jesus took the cup after supper, saying, "This cup is the new covenant in My blood, which is shed for you."

Luke 22:35-38

Supplies for the Road

And Jesus said to them, "When I sent you without money bag, knapsack, and sandals, did you lack anything?"

So, they said, "Nothing."

Then He said to them, "But now, he who has a money bag, let him take it, and likewise a knapsack; and he who has no sword, let him sell some of his clothes and buy one. For I say to you, what is written must still be accomplished in Me: *'And He was numbered with the transgressors.'* For the things concerning Me have an end."

So, they said, "Lord, look, here are two swords."

And He said to them, "It is enough."

John 14:1-24

The Way, the Truth, and the Life

Jesus continued, "Let not your heart be troubled; you believe in God, believe also in Me. In My Father's house are many mansions;

if it were not so, I would have told you. I go to prepare a place for you. And if I go and prepare a place for you, I will come again and receive you to Myself; that where I am, there you may be also. And where I go you know, and the way you know."

Thomas said to Him, "Lord, we do not know where You are going, and how can we know the way?"

Jesus said to him, "I am the way, the truth, and the life. No one comes to the Father except through Me.

The Father Revealed

"If you had known Me, you would have known My Father also; and from now on you know Him and have seen Him."

Philip said to Him, "Lord, show us the Father, and it is sufficient for us."

Jesus said to him, "Have I been with you so long, and yet you have not known Me, Philip? He who has seen Me has seen the Father; so how can you say, 'Show us the Father'? Do you not believe that I am in the Father, and the Father in Me? The words that I speak to you I do not speak on My own authority; but the Father who dwells in Me does the works. Believe Me that I am in the Father and the Father in Me, or else believe Me for the sake of the works themselves."

The Answered Prayer

Jesus continued, "I say to you, he who believes in Me, the works that I do he will do also; and greater works than these he will do, because I go to My Father. And whatever you ask in My name, that I will do, that the Father may be glorified in the Son. If you ask anything in My name, I will do it.

Jesus Promises Another Helper

"If you love Me, keep My commandments. And I will pray the Father, and He will give you another Helper, that He may abide with you forever, the Spirit of truth, whom the world cannot receive, because it neither sees Him nor knows Him; but you know Him, for He dwells with you and will be in you. I will not leave you orphans; I will come to you.

Indwelling of the Father and the Son

"A little while longer and the world will see Me no more, but you will see Me. Because I live, you will live also. At that day, you will know that I am in My Father, and you in Me, and I in you. He who has My commandments and keeps them, it is he who loves Me. And he who loves Me will be loved by My Father, and I will love him and make Myself known to him."

Judas (not Iscariot) said to Him, "Lord, how is it that You will make Yourself known to us, and not to the world?"

Jesus answered and said to him, "If anyone loves Me, he will keep My word; and My Father will love him, and We will come to him and make Our home with him. He who does not love Me does not keep My words; and the word which you hear is not Mine but the Father who sent Me.

John 14:25 to 16:33

The Gift of His Peace

"These things I have spoken to you while being present with you. But the Helper, the Holy Spirit, whom the Father will send in My name, He will teach you all things, and bring to your remembrance all things that I said to you. Peace I leave with you, My peace I give to you; not as the world gives do I give to you. Let not your heart be troubled, neither let it be afraid. You have heard Me say to you, 'I am going away and coming back to you.' If you loved Me, you would rejoice because I said, 'I am going to the Father,' for My Father is greater than I.

"And now I have told you before it comes, that when it does come to pass, you may believe. I will no longer talk much with you, for the ruler of this world is coming, and he has nothing in Me. But that the world may know that I love the Father, and as the Father gave Me commandment, so I do.

The True Vine

"I am the true vine, and My Father is the vinedresser. Every branch in Me that does not bear fruit He takes away; and every branch that bears fruit He prunes, that it may bear more fruit. You are already clean because of the word which I have spoken to you. Abide in Me, and I in you. As the branch cannot bear fruit of itself, unless it is part of the vine, neither can you, unless you are a part of Me.

"I am the vine, you are the branches. He who is part of Me, and I in him, supports much fruit; for without Me you can do nothing. If anyone does not become part of Me, he is cast out as a branch and is withered; and they gather them and throw them into the fire, and they are burned. If you are part of Me, and My words are in you, you will ask what you desire, and it shall be done for you. By this My Father is glorified, that you support much fruit; so, you will be My disciples.

Love and Joy Perfected

"As the Father loved Me, I also have loved you; stay in My love. If you keep My commandments, you will stay in My love, just as I have kept My Father's commandments and stay in His love.

"These things I have spoken to you, that My joy may remain in you, and that your joy may be full. This is My commandment, that you love one another as I have loved you. Greater love has no one than this, than to lay down one's life for his friends. You are My friends if you do whatever I command you. No longer do I call you servants, for a servant does not know what his master is doing; but I have called you friends, for all things that I heard from My Father I have made known to you. You did not choose Me, but I chose you and appointed you that you should go and support my fruit, and that your fruit should remain, that whatever you ask the Father in My name He may give you. These things I command you, that you love one another.

The World's Hatred

"If the world hates you, you know that it hated Me before it hated you. If you were of the world, the world would love its own. Yet because you are not of the world, but I chose you out of the world, then the world hates you. Remember the word that I said to you, 'A servant is not greater than his master.' If they persecuted Me, they will also persecute you. If they kept My word, they will keep yours also. But all these things they will do to you for My name's sake, because they do not know Him who sent Me. If I had not come and spoken to them, they would have no sin, but now they have no excuse for their sin. He who hates Me hates My Father also. If I had not done among them the works which no one else did, they would have no sin; but now they have seen and also hated both Me and My Father. But this happened that the word might be fulfilled which is written in their law, *'They hated Me without a cause.'*

The Coming Rejection

"But when the Helper comes, whom I shall send to you from the Father, the Spirit of truth who proceeds from the Father, He will testify of Me. And you also will bear witness, because you have been with Me from the beginning.

Jesus Warns and Comforts His Disciples

"These things I have spoken to you, that you should not be made to stumble. They will put you out of the synagogues; yes, the time is coming that whoever kills you will think that he offers God service. And these things they will do to you because they have not known the Father or Me. But these things I have told you, that when the time comes, you may remember that I told you of them. And these things I did not say to you at the beginning, because I was with you.

The Work of the Holy Spirit

"But now I go away to Him who sent Me, and none of you asks Me, 'Where are You going?' But because I have said these things to you, sorrow has filled your heart. I tell you the truth. It is to your advantage that I go away; for if I do not go away, the Helper will not come to you; but if I depart, I will send Him to you. And when He has come, He will convict the world of sin, and of righteousness, and of judgment: of sin, because they do not believe in Me; of righteousness, because I go to My Father and you see Me no more; of judgment, because the ruler of this world is judged.

"I still have many things to say to you, but you cannot bear them now. However, when He, the Spirit of truth, has come, He will guide you into all truth; for He will not speak on His own authority, but whatever He hears He will speak; and He will tell you things to come. He will glorify Me, for He will take of what is Mine and declare it to you. All things that the Father has are Mine. Therefore, I said that He will take of Mine and tell it to you.

Sorrow Will Turn to Joy

"A little while, and you will not see Me; and again, a little while, and you will see Me, because I go to the Father."

Then some of His disciples said among themselves, "What is this that He says to us, 'A little while, and you will not see Me; and again, a little while, and you will see Me'; and, 'because I go to the Father'?" They said therefore, "What is this that He says, 'A little while'? We do not know what He is saying."

Now Jesus knew that they desired to ask Him, and He said to them, "Are you inquiring among yourselves about what I said, 'A little while, and you will not see Me; and again, a little while, and you will see Me'? I say to you that you will weep and be sorrowful, but the world will rejoice; and you will be sorrowful, but your sorrow will be turned into joy. A woman, when she is in labour, has sorrow because her hour has come; but as soon as she has given birth to the child, she no longer remembers the pain, for joy that a human being has been born into the world. Therefore, you now have sorrow; but I will see you again and your heart will rejoice, and your joy no one will take from you.

"And in that day, you will ask Me nothing. I say to you, whatever you ask the Father in My name He will give you. Until now you have asked nothing in My name. Ask, and you will receive, that your joy may be full.

Jesus Christ Has Overcome the World

"These things I have spoken to you in figurative language; but the time is coming when I will no longer speak to you in figurative language, but I will tell you plainly about the Father. In that day, you will ask in My name, and I do not say to you that I shall pray the Father for you; for the Father Himself loves you, because you have loved Me, and have believed that I was sent from God. I came from the Father and have come into the world. Again, I leave the world and go to the Father."

His disciples said to Him, "See, now You are speaking plainly, and using no figure of speech! Now we are sure that You know all things, and have no need that anyone should question You. By this we believe that You came from God."

Jesus answered them, "Do you now believe? I tell you, the hour is coming, yes, has now come, that you will be scattered, each to his own, and will leave Me alone. And yet I am not alone, because the Father is with Me. These things I have spoken to you, that in Me you may have peace. In the world, you will have tribulation; but be of good cheer, I have overcome the world."

John 17:1-26

Jesus Prays for Himself

Jesus spoke these words, lifted up His eyes to heaven, and said: "Father, the hour has come. Glorify Your Son, that Your Son also may glorify You, as You have given Him authority over all flesh, that He should give eternal life to as many as You have given Him. And this is eternal life, that they may know You, the only true God, and Jesus Christ whom You have sent. I have glorified You on the earth. I have finished the work which You have given Me to do. And now, O Father, glorify Me together with Yourself, with the glory which I had with You before the world was.

Jesus Prays for His Disciples

"I have made known Your name to the men whom You have given Me out of the world. They were Yours, You gave them to Me, and they have kept Your word. Now they have known that all things which You have given Me are from You. For I have given to them the words which You have given Me; and they have received them, and have known that I came from You; and they have believed that You sent Me.

"I pray for them. I do not pray for the world but for those whom You have given Me, for they are Yours. And all Mine are Yours, and Yours are Mine, and I am glorified in them. Now I am no longer in the world, but these are in the world, and I come to You. Holy Father, keep through Your name those whom You have given Me, that they may be one as We are. While I was with them in the world, I kept them in Your name. Those whom You gave Me I have kept; and none of them is lost except the son of perdition, that the Scripture might be fulfilled. But now I come to You, and these things I speak in the world, that they may have My joy fulfilled in themselves. I have given them Your word; and the world has hated them because they are not of the world, just as I am not of the world. I do not pray that You should take them out of the world, but that You should keep them from the evil one. They are not of the world, just as I am not of the world. Sanctify them by Your truth. Your word is truth. As You sent Me into the world, I also have sent them into the world. And for their sakes I sanctify Myself, that they also may be sanctified by the truth.

Jesus Prays for All Believers

"I do not pray for these alone, but also for those who will believe in Me through their word; that they all may be one, as You, Father, are in Me, and I in You; that they also may be one in Us, that the world may believe that You sent Me. And the glory which You gave Me I have given them, that they may be one just as We are one: I in them, and You in Me; that they may be made perfect in one, and that the world may know that You have sent Me, and have loved them as You have loved Me.

"Father, I desire that they also whom You gave Me may be with Me where I am, that they may behold My glory which You have given Me; for You loved Me before the foundation of the world. O righteous Father! The world has not known You, but I have known You; and these have known that You sent Me. And I have declared to them Your name, and will declare it, that the love with which You loved Me may be in them, and I in them."

Matthew 26:36-56, Mark 14:26, 32-52, Luke 22:39-53, John 18:1-11

The Prayer in the Garden

And when Jesus and the disciples had sung a hymn, they went out to the Mount of Olives. This was a custom of Jesus, and His disciples also followed Him. As they went, Jesus crossed over the Kidron Brook. Then they came to a place where there was a garden, which was named Gethsemane, which Jesus and His disciples entered.

And He said to His disciples, "Sit here and pray that you may not enter into temptation."

And He took Peter and the two sons of Zebedee, James, and John with Him, and He began to be troubled and deeply distressed.

Then He said to them, "My soul is extremely sorrowful, even to death. Stay here and watch with Me."

He went a little further, about a stone's throw, and fell on His face, and prayed that if it were possible, the hour might pass from Him. And He said, "Abba, Father, all things are possible for You. Take this cup away from Me; nevertheless, not what I will, but what You will."

Then an angel appeared to Him from heaven, strengthening Him. And being in agony, He prayed more earnestly. Then His sweat became like great drops of blood falling down to the ground.

When He rose up from prayer, and came to His disciples, He found them sleeping from sorrow.

Then He said to them, "Why do you sleep? Wake up and pray, unless you enter into temptation. Simon, are you sleeping? Could you not watch with Me one hour? Watch and pray, or you enter into temptation. The spirit is willing, but the flesh is weak."

Again, He went away and prayed, saying, "O My Father, if this cup cannot pass away from Me unless I drink it, Your will be done."

And when He returned, He found them asleep again, for their eyes were heavy; and they did not know what to answer Him.

So, He left them, went away again, and prayed the third time, saying the same words.

Then He came to His disciples and said to them, "Are you still sleeping and resting? It is enough! Behold, the hour is at hand, and the Son of Man is being betrayed into the hands of sinners. Stand up and let us be going. See, My betrayer is at hand."

Betrayal and Arrest in Gethsemane

Judas, who betrayed Jesus, also knew this place; for Jesus often met there with His disciples. Then Judas, having received a detachment of troops, and officers from the chief priests and Pharisees, came there with lanterns, torches, and weapons.

Jesus, knowing all things that would happen to Him, went forward and said to them, "Whom are you seeking?"

They answered Him, "Jesus of Nazareth."

Jesus said to them, "I am He."

And Judas, who betrayed Him, also stood with them. Now when He said to them, "I am He," they drew back and fell to the ground.

Then He asked them again, "Whom are you seeking?"

And they said, "Jesus of Nazareth."

Jesus answered, "I have told you that I am He. If you seek Me, let these go their way."

He said this that the saying might be fulfilled which He spoke, "Of those whom You gave Me I have lost none."

Now His betrayer had given them a sign, saying, "Whomever I kiss, He is the One; seize Him." Immediately he went up to Jesus and said, "Greetings, Rabbi!" and kissed Him.

But Jesus said to him, "Friend, why have you come? Are you betraying the Son of Man with a kiss?"

Then they came and laid hands on Jesus and took Him.

When those around Him saw what was going to happen, they said to Him, "Lord, shall we strike with the sword?"

And suddenly, Simon Peter, having a sword, drew it and struck the high priest's servant, and cut off his right ear. The servant's name was Malchus.

So, Jesus said to Peter, "Put your sword into the sheath. Shall I not drink the cup which My Father has given Me?"

Then Jesus said, "Permit even this."

And He touched his ear and healed him.

Jesus said to Peter, "Put your sword in its place, for all who take the sword will perish by the sword. Or do you think that I cannot now pray to My Father, and He will provide Me with more than twelve legions of angels? How then could the Scriptures be fulfilled, that it must happen this way?"

Then Jesus said to the chief priests, captains of the temple, and the elders who came to Him, "Have you come out, as against a robber, with swords and clubs? When I was with you daily in the temple, you did not try to seize Me. But this is your hour, and the power of darkness."

But all this was done that the Scriptures of the prophets might be fulfilled.

Then all the disciples abandoned Him and fled.

A Young Man Flees Naked

Now a certain young man followed Him, having a linen cloth thrown around his naked body. And the young men laid hold of him, and he left the linen cloth and fled from them naked.

Matthew 26:57-75, Mark 14:53-72, Luke 22:54-71, John 18:12-27

Jesus Faces the Sanhedrin

And those who had laid hold of Jesus led Him away to Caiaphas the high priest, and with him were assembled all the chief priests, the elders, and the scribes. But Peter followed Him at a distance, right into the courtyard of the high priest, where he sat with the servants and warmed himself at the fire, waiting to see the end.

Now the chief priests, the elders, and all the council sought false testimony against Jesus to put Him to death, but found none.

Even though many bore false witness against Him, and came forward, their testimonies did not agree. As soon as it was day, the elders of the people, both chief priests and scribes, came together and led Him into their council. At last two false witnesses came forward and said, "We heard Him say, 'I will destroy this temple made with hands, and within three days I will build another made without hands.'"

And the high priest stood up and said to Jesus, "Do You answer nothing? What is it these men testify against You?"

But Jesus kept silent and answered nothing.

Then the high priest said to Him, "I put You under oath by the living God: Tell us if You are the Christ, the Son of the Blessed, the Son of God!"

Jesus said to them, "If I tell you, you will by no means believe. And if I also ask you, you will by no means answer Me or let Me go. Hereafter the Son of Man will sit on the right hand of the power of God and coming on the clouds of heaven."

Then they all said, "Are You then the Son of God?"

So, He said to them, "You rightly say that I am."

Then the high priest tore his clothes, saying, "He has spoken blasphemy! What further need do we have of witnesses? Look, now you have heard His blasphemy! What do you think?"

And they said, "What further testimony do we need? For we have heard it ourselves from His own mouth. He is deserving of death."

Then they spat in His face, blindfolded Him and beat Him; and others struck Him with the palms of their hands, saying, "Prophesy to us, Christ! Who is the one who struck You?"

Peter Denies Jesus, and Weeps Bitterly

Simon Peter, along with another disciple had followed Jesus. Now the other disciple was known to the high priest, and went with Jesus into the courtyard of the high priest. But Peter stood outside the door, below in the courtyard. Then the other disciple, who was known to the high priest, went out and spoke to her who kept the door, and brought Peter in.

Now the servants and officers who had made a fire of coals stood there, for it was cold, and they warmed themselves. And Peter stood with them and warmed himself.

And one of the servant girls of the high priest, a relative of him whose ear Peter cut off, said, "You also were with Jesus of Galilee. Did I not see you in the garden with Him?"

But Peter denied it before them all, saying, "I neither know or understand what you are saying."

And when he had gone out to the gateway, another girl saw him and said to those who were there, "This fellow also was with Jesus of Nazareth."

But again, he denied with an oath, "I do not know the Man!" and a rooster crowed.

After about an hour had passed, Peter went out onto the porch.

Those who stood by came up and said to Peter, "Surely you are one of them, for you are a Galilean, for your speech betrays you."

Then he began to curse and swear, saying, "I do not know the Man of whom you speak!"

Immediately, while he was still speaking, the rooster crowed a second time. And the Lord turned and looked at Peter. Then Peter called to mind, remembered the words of Jesus who had said to him, "Before the rooster crows twice, you will deny Me three times." So, Peter went out and wept bitterly.

Before the High Priest

Then the detachment of troops and the captain and the officers of the Jews arrested Jesus and bound Him. And they led Him away to Annas first, for he was the father-in-law of Caiaphas who was high priest that year. Now it was Caiaphas who advised the Jews that it was necessary that one man should die for the people.

Jesus Questioned by the High Priest

The high priest then asked Jesus about His disciples and His doctrine.

Jesus answered him, "I spoke openly to the world. I always taught in synagogues and in the temple, where the Jews always meet, and in secret I have said nothing. Why do you ask Me? Ask those who have heard Me what I said to them. They know what I said."

And when He had said these things, one of the officers who stood by struck Jesus with the palm of his hand, saying, "Do You answer the high priest like that?"

Jesus answered him, "If I have spoken evil, bear witness of the evil; but if not, why do you strike Me?"

Then Annas sent Him bound, back to Caiaphas the high priest.

Matthew 27:1-26, Mark 15:1-15, Luke 23:1-25, John 18:28-40

Jesus Handed Over to Pontius Pilate

When morning came, all the chief priests and elders of the people plotted against Jesus to put Him to death. And when they had bound Him, they led Jesus away and delivered Him to Pontius Pilate the governor.

Judas Hangs Himself

Then Judas, Jesus betrayer, seeing Jesus had been condemned, was remorseful and brought back the thirty pieces of silver to the chief priests and elders, saying, "I have sinned by betraying innocent blood."

And they said, "What is that to us? You see to it!"

Then Judas threw down the pieces of silver in the temple and departed, and went and hanged himself.

But the chief priests took the silver pieces and said, "It is not lawful to put them into the treasury, because they are the price of blood."

And they consulted together and bought with them the potter's field, to bury strangers in. For that reason, that field has been called the Field of Blood to this day.

This fulfilled what was spoken by Jeremiah the prophet, saying, *"And they took the thirty pieces of silver, the value of Him who was priced,* whom they of the children of Israel priced, *and gave them for the potter's field, as the Lord directed me."*

Jesus Faces Pilate

Having delivered Jesus to Pilate, the Priests did not go into the Praetorium, because they would be unclean and not be able to eat the Passover. Pilate then went out to them and said, "What accusation do you bring against this Man?"

They answered and said to him, "If He were not an evildoer, we would not have delivered Him up to you." And they began to accuse Him, saying, "We found this fellow perverting the nation, and forbidding to pay taxes to Caesar, saying that He Himself is Christ, a King."

Then Pilate said to them, "You take Him and judge Him according to your law."

The Jews said to him, "It is not lawful for us to put anyone to death," that the saying of Jesus might be fulfilled which He spoke, signifying by what death He would die.

Then Pilate entered the Praetorium, called Jesus, and said to Him, "Are You the King of the Jews?"

Jesus answered him, "Are you speaking for yourself about this, or did others tell you this concerning Me?"

Pilate answered, "Am I a Jew? Your own nation and the chief priests have delivered You to me. What have You done?"

Jesus answered, "My kingdom is not of this world. If My kingdom were of this world, My servants would fight, so that I should not be delivered to the Jews; but now My kingdom is not from here."

Pilate, for this reason said to Him, "Are You a king then?"

Jesus answered, "You say rightly that I am a king. For this cause I was born, and for this cause I have come into the world, that I should bear witness to the truth. Everyone who is of the truth hears My voice."

Pilate said to Him, "What is truth?"

And the chief priests accused Him of many things, but He answered nothing.

Then Pilate asked Him again, saying, "Do You answer nothing? See how many things they testify against You!"

But Jesus still answered nothing, so that Pilate marvelled. And when he had said this, Pilate went out again to the Jews, and said to them, "I find no fault in Him at all. But the Priests were the more fierce, saying, "He stirs up the people, teaching throughout all Judea, beginning from Galilee to this place."

Jesus Faces Herod

When Pilate heard of Galilee, he asked if the Man were a Galilean. And as soon as he knew that He belonged to Herod's jurisdiction, he sent Jesus to Herod, who was also in Jerusalem at that time.

Now when Herod saw Jesus, he was extremely glad; for he had desired for a long time to see Him, because he had heard many things about Him, and he hoped to see some miracle done by Him. Then Herod questioned Jesus with many words, but He answered him nothing. And the chief priests and scribes angrily stood nearby, passionately accusing Him. Then Herod, with his men of war, treated Him with contempt and mocked Him, arrayed Him in a gorgeous robe, and sent Him back to Pilate. That very day Pilate and Herod became friends with each other, for previously they had been hostile with each other.

Taking the Place of Barabbas

Then Pilate, when he had called together the chief priests, the rulers, and the people, said to them, "You have brought this Man to me, as one who misleads the people. Having examined Him in your presence, I have found no fault in this Man concerning those things of which you accuse Him; no, neither did Herod, for I sent you back to him; nothing deserving of death has been done by Him. I will therefore chastise Him and release Him".

Now at the feast of the Passover, the governor was accustomed to releasing to the multitude one prisoner whom they wished. And at that time, they had a notorious prisoner called Barabbas. So, when they had gathered together, Pilate said to them, "Whom do you want me to release to you? Barabbas, or Jesus who is called Christ?" For he knew they had handed Him over because of envy.

While he was sitting on the judgment seat, his wife sent to him, saying, "Have nothing to do with this just Man, for I have suffered many things today in a dream because of Him."

But the chief priests and elders persuaded the multitudes that they should ask for Barabbas and destroy Jesus.

The governor answered and said to them, "Which of the two do you want me to release to you? Do you want me to release to you the King of the Jews?"

Then they all cried again, saying, "Not this Man, but Barabbas!" And they all cried out at once, saying, "Away with this Man, and release to us Barabbas".

Now Barabbas was in prison chained with his fellow rebels; they had committed murder in the rebellion. Pilate, wishing to release Jesus, again called out to them. But the chief priests stirred up the crowd.

They shouted, "Crucify Him, crucify Him!"

Then he said to them the third time, "Why, what evil has He done? I have found no fault or reason why this man should be put to death. I will therefore chastise Him and let Him go."

But they were insistent, demanding with loud voices that He be crucified. And the voices of these men and of the chief priests proved more powerful.

When Pilate saw that he could not persuade them at all, but rather that a loud confused noise was increasing, he took water and washed his hands before the multitude, saying, "I am innocent of the blood of this just Person. You see to it."

And all the people answered and said, "His blood be on us and on our children."

So, Pilate gave sentence that it should be as they requested. Then he released Barabbas to them, and Jesus to the soldiers to have Him scourged.

Matthew 27:27-31, Mark 15:16-20, John 19:1-16

The Soldiers Mock Jesus

Then the soldiers of the governor took Jesus into the Praetorium and gathered the whole garrison around Him.

And they stripped Jesus and scourged Him. When the soldiers had twisted a crown of thorns, they put it on His head, and a reed in His right hand, and put a scarlet robe on Him. And they bowed the knee before Jesus and mocked Him, saying, "Hail, King of the Jews!" Then they spat on Him, and took the reed and struck Him on the head. And when they had mocked Him, they took the robe off Him, and put His own clothes on Him.

Pilate then went out again, and said to them, "Behold, I am bringing Him out to you, that you may know that I find no fault in Him."

Pilate's Decision

Then Jesus came out, wearing the crown of thorns and the purple robe. And Pilate said to them, "Behold the Man!"

Therefore, when the chief priests and officers saw Jesus, they cried out, saying, "Crucify Him, crucify Him!"

Pilate said to them, "You take Him and crucify Him, for I find no fault in Him."

The Jews answered him, "We have a law, and according to our law He ought to die, because He made Himself the Son of God."

For this reason, when Pilate heard that saying, he was the more afraid, and went again into the Praetorium, and said to Jesus, "Where are You from?"

But Jesus gave him no answer.

Then Pilate said to Him, "Are You not speaking to me? Do You not know that I have power to crucify You, and power to release You?"

Jesus answered, "You could have no power at all against Me unless it had been given to you from above. Therefore, the one who delivered Me to you has the greater sin."

From then on Pilate wanted to release Him, but the Jews cried out, saying, "If you let this Man go, you are not Caesar's friend. Whoever makes himself a king speaks against Caesar."

When Pilate heard that saying, he brought Jesus out and sat down in the judgment seat in a place that is called The Pavement, but in Hebrew, Gabbatha. Now it was the Preparation Day of the Passover, and about the sixth hour. And he said to the Jews, "Behold your King!"

But the crowd cried out, "Away with Him, away with Him! Crucify Him!"

Pilate said to them, "Shall I crucify your King?"

The chief priests answered, "We have no king but Caesar!"

Then he delivered Jesus to them to be crucified. Then they took Jesus and led Him away.

Matthew 27:32-56, Mark 15:21-41, Luke 23:26-49, John 19:17-37

The King on a Cross

Now as the soldiers led Jesus away, they laid hold of a certain man, Simon a Cyrenian, the father of Alexander and Rufus, who was coming from the country, and compelled him to carry Jesus' cross, and on him they laid the cross that he might carry it after Jesus.

And a great multitude of the people followed Him, and women who also mourned and passionately grieved for Him.

But Jesus, turning to them, said, "Daughters of Jerusalem, do not weep for Me, but weep for yourselves and for your children.

For the days are coming in which they will say, 'Blessed are the barren, wombs that never bore children, and breasts which never nursed!' Then they will begin to *say to the mountains, "Fall on us!"* and to the hills, *"Cover us!"'* For if they do these things in the green wood, what will be done in the dry?"

And He, went out to a place called the Place of a Skull, which is called in Hebrew, Golgotha, and there they gave Jesus sour wine mingled with gall to drink. But when He had tasted it, He would not drink.

Then they crucified Him, and two others with Him, one on either side, and Jesus in the centre. Now Pilate wrote a title and put it on the cross. And the writing was:

*THIS IS JESUS THE KING
OF THE JEWS.*

Then many of the Jews read this title, for the place where Jesus was crucified was near the city; and it was written in Hebrew, Greek, and Latin.

Therefore, the chief priests of the Jews said to Pilate, "Do not write, 'The King of the Jews,' but, 'He said, "I am the King of the Jews."'"

Pilate answered, "What I have written, I have written."

Now it was the third hour, the soldiers, sitting down, kept watch over Him there. Then the soldiers took His garments and made four parts, to each soldier a part, and also the tunic. Now the robe was without seam, woven from the top in one piece. They said therefore among themselves, "Let us not tear it, but cast lots for it, whose it shall be," that the Scripture might be fulfilled which says:

"They divided My garments among them,
And for My clothing they cast lots,"

then the soldiers did these things.

And the people stood looking on. Even the rulers with them sneered, saying, "He saved others; let Him save Himself if He is the Christ, the chosen of God." The soldiers also mocked Him, coming and offering Him sour wine, and saying, "If You are the King of the Jews, save Yourself."

Jesus said, "Father, forgive them, for they do not know what they do."

With Him they crucified two robbers, one on His right and the other on His left, so the Scripture was fulfilled which says, *"And He was numbered with the transgressors."*

Then one of the criminals who was being crucified, blasphemed Him, saying, "If You are the Christ, save Yourself and us."

But the other, answering, rebuked him, saying, "Do you not even fear God, seeing you are under the same condemnation? And we justly, for we receive the due reward of our deeds; but this Man has done nothing wrong." Then he said to Jesus, "Lord, remember me when You come into Your kingdom."

And Jesus said to him, "I say to you, today you will be with Me in Paradise."

And those who passed by blasphemed Him, wagging their heads and saying, "You who destroy the temple and build it in three days, save Yourself! If You are the Son of God, come down from the cross. Let the Christ, the King of Israel, descend now from the cross, that we may see and believe Him, for You said, 'I am the Son of God.'"

The Death of Jesus

Now it was about the sixth hour, and the sun was darkened and there was darkness over all the earth until the ninth hour.

Behold Your Mother

Now there stood by the cross of Jesus His mother, and His mother's sister Salome, Mary the wife of Clopas, and Mary Magdalene.

When Jesus saw His mother, and the disciple whom He loved standing by, He said to His mother, "Woman, behold your son!" Then He said to the disciple, "Behold your mother!"

And from that hour that disciple took her to his own home.

Jesus Dies on the Cross

And about the ninth hour Jesus cried out with a loud voice, saying, "Eloi, Eloi, lama sabachthani?" which is translated, *"My God, My God, why have You forsaken Me?"*

Some of those who stood by, when they heard that, said, "Look, He is calling for Elijah!" Then someone ran and filled a sponge full of sour wine, put it on a reed, and offered it to Him to drink. But a bystander said, "Let Him alone; let us see if Elijah will come to take Him down."

Now Jesus cried out with a loud voice and said, *"Father, into Your hands I commit My spirit."*

It Is Finished

After this, Jesus, knowing that all things were now accomplished, that the Scripture might be fulfilled, said, "I thirst!"

Now a vessel full of sour wine was sitting there; and they filled a sponge with sour wine, put it on hyssop, and put it to His mouth.

So, when Jesus had received the sour wine, He said, "It is finished!" And bowing His head, He gave up His spirit.

Then, the veil of the temple was torn in two from top to bottom; and the earth quaked, and the rocks were split, and the graves were opened; and many bodies of the saints who had fallen asleep were raised; and coming out of the graves after His resurrection, they went into the holy city and appeared to many.

So, when the centurion and those with him, who were guarding Jesus, felt the earthquake and saw the things that had happened, they feared greatly, saying, "Certainly this was a righteous Man! Truly this was the Son of God!"

And many women who followed Jesus from Galilee, ministering to Him, were there looking on from a distance, among whom were Mary Magdalene, Mary the mother of James and Joses, and Salome, the mother of Zebedee's sons and many other women who came up with Him from Jerusalem. And the whole crowd who came together to that sight, seeing what had been done, displayed their grief in a loud manner and returned.

Jesus' Side Is Pierced

Now, because it was the Preparation Day, it was required the bodies should not remain on the cross on the Sabbath (for that Sabbath was a high day). The Jews asked Pilate that their legs might be broken, and that they might be taken away. Then the soldiers came and broke the legs of the first and of the other who was crucified with Jesus. But when they came to Jesus and saw that He was already dead, they did not break His legs. But one of the soldiers pierced Jesus side with a spear, and immediately blood and water came out.

He who has seen has testified, and his testimony is true; and he knows that he is telling the truth, so that you may believe. For these things were done that the Scripture should be fulfilled, *"Not one of His bones shall be broken."* And again, another Scripture says, *"They shall look on Him whom they pierced."*

Matthew 27:57-66, Mark 15:42-47, Luke 23:50-56, John 19:38-42

Jesus Buried in a Tomb

Now when evening had come, because it was the Preparation Day, that is, the day before the Sabbath, Joseph of Arimathea, a disciple of Jesus, but secretly, for fear of the Jews, a prominent council member, a good and just man, who was himself waiting for the kingdom of God, coming and taking courage, went in to Pilate and asked for the body of Jesus. Joseph of Arimathea had not consented to their decision and deed. Pilate marvelled that Jesus was already dead; and summoning the centurion, he asked him if He had been dead for some time. So, when he found out from the centurion, he granted the body to Joseph. Then Joseph bought fine linen, took Him down, and wrapped Him in the clean linen cloth.

Nicodemus, who first came to Jesus by night, also came, bringing a mixture of myrrh and aloes, about a hundred pounds. Then they took the body of Jesus, and bound it in strips of linen with the spices, as the custom of the Jews is to bury. Now in the place where Jesus was crucified there was a garden, and in the garden a new tomb in which no one had yet been laid. So, there they laid Jesus, because of the Jews' Preparation Day, for the tomb was nearby. Then they laid Him in the tomb which had been carved out of the rock, and rolled a large stone against the door of the tomb and departed.

And the women who came with Jesus from Galilee followed after, and they observed the tomb and how His body was laid. And Mary Magdalene and Mary the mother of Joses, sitting opposite the tomb, observed where He was laid. Then they returned and prepared spices and fragrant oils. And they rested on the Sabbath according to the commandment.

Pilate Sets a Guard

On the next day, which followed the Day of Preparation, the chief priests and Pharisees gathered together to Pilate, saying, "Sir, we remember, while Jesus was still alive, how that deceiver said, 'After three days I will rise.' Therefore, command that the tomb be made secure until the third day, lest His disciples come by night and steal Him away, and say to the people, 'He has risen from the dead.' So, the last deception will be worse than the first."

Pilate said to them, "You have a guard; go your way, make it as secure as you know how."

So, they went and made the tomb secure, sealing the stone and setting the guard.

Matthew 28:1-3, Mark 16:9-11, John 20:1, 11-18

Mary Magdalene Sees the Risen Lord

Now after the Sabbath, the first day of the week before the dawn, there was a great earthquake; for an angel of the Lord descended from heaven, and came and rolled back the stone from the door, and sat on it. His countenance was like lightning, and his clothing as white as snow. And the guards shook for fear of him, and became like dead men.

Now when Jesus rose on the first day of the week, He appeared first to Mary Magdalene, out of whom He had cast seven demons. Mary Magdalene had gone early to the tomb, while it was still dark, and saw that the stone had been taken away from the tomb entrance. Mary stood outside by the tomb weeping, and as she wept she bent down and looked into the tomb. And she saw two angels in white sitting, one at the head and the other at the feet, where the body of Jesus had lain. Then they said to her, "Woman, why are you weeping?"

She said to them, "Because they have taken away my Lord, and I do not know where they have laid Him."

Now when she had said this, she turned around and saw Jesus standing there, and did not know that it was Jesus.

Jesus said to her, "Woman, why are you weeping? Whom are you seeking?"

She, supposing Him to be the gardener, said to Him, "Sir, if You have carried Him away, tell me where You have laid Him, and I will take Him away."

Jesus said to her, "Mary!"

She looked at Him and said, "Rabboni!" (which is to say, Teacher).

Jesus said to her, "Do not cling to Me, for I have not yet ascended to My Father; but go to My brothers and say to them, 'I am ascending to My Father and your Father, and to My God and your God.'"

Mary Magdalene came and told the disciples that she had seen the Lord, and that He had spoken these things to her. She said, "The angels told me to tell you. They said, 'Go, tell His disciples, and Peter, that He is going before you into Galilee; there you will see Him, as He said to you.'"

Matthew 28:4-15, Mark 16:1-8, Luke 24:1-12, John 20:2-10

He Is Risen

Now when the Sabbath was past, Mary the mother of James, and Salome bought spices, that they might come and anoint the body of Jesus. Very early in the morning, on the first day of the week, they came to the tomb when the sun had risen. And they said among themselves, "Who will roll away the stone from the door of the tomb for us?"

But when they looked up, they saw that the stone had been rolled away, for it was very large. And entering the tomb, they saw a young man clothed in a long white robe sitting on the right side; and they were alarmed.

Then two men stood by them in shining garments. The women were afraid and bowed their faces to the earth, but they said to them, "Do not be alarmed. You seek Jesus of Nazareth, who was crucified. Why do you seek the living among the dead? He is not here, but is risen! Remember how He spoke to you when He was still in Galilee, saying, 'The Son of Man must be delivered into the hands of sinful men, and be crucified, and the third day rise again.'" And they remembered His words.

The Women Worship the Risen Lord

And as the women went to tell His disciples, Jesus met them, saying, "Rejoice!" So, they came and held Him by the feet and worshiped Him.

Then Jesus said to them, "Do not be afraid. Go and tell My brothers to go to Galilee, and there they will see Me."

Then they returned from the tomb and told all these things to the eleven and to all the rest. It was Mary Magdalene, Joanna, Mary the mother of James, and the other women with them, who told these things to the apostles. And their words seemed to them like idle tales, and they did not believe them.

Peter then went out, and the other disciple, and were going to the tomb. So, they both ran together, and the other disciple outran Peter and came to the tomb first. And he, stooping down and looking in, saw the linen cloths lying there; yet he did not go in. Then Simon Peter came, following him, and went into the tomb; and he saw the linen cloths lying there, and the handkerchief that had been around His head, not with the linen cloths, but folded together in a place by itself. Then the other disciple, who came to the tomb first, went in also; and he saw and believed. For as yet they did not know the Scripture, that He must rise again from the dead.

Then the disciples went away again to their own homes.

The Soldiers Are Bribed

Now while Peter and the other disciple were going to the tomb, some of the guard came into the city and reported to the chief priests all the things that had happened.

When they had assembled with the elders and consulted together, they gave a large sum of money to the soldiers, saying, "Tell them, 'His disciples came at night and stole Him away while we slept.' And if this comes to the governor's ears, we will appease him and make you secure."

So, they took the money and did as they were instructed; and this saying is commonly reported among the Jews until this day.

Mark 16:12-13, Luke 24:13-49, John 20:19-31

Jesus Appears to Two on The Road to Emmaus

After that, Jesus appeared in another form to two of them as they walked and went into the country, that same day to a village called Emmaus, which was seven miles from Jerusalem. And they talked together of all these things which had happened. It was while they talked, shared and reasoned, that Jesus Himself came near and went with them. But their eyes were restrained, so that they did not know Him.

And He said to them, "What kind of conversation is this that you have with one another as you walk and are sad?"

Then the one whose name was Cleopas answered and said to Him, "Are You the only stranger in Jerusalem, and have You not known the things which happened there in these days?"

And He said to them, "What things?"

So, they said to Him, "The things concerning Jesus of Nazareth, who was a Prophet mighty in deed and word before God and all the people, and how the chief priests and our rulers delivered Him to be condemned to death, and crucified Him. But we were hoping that it was He who was going to redeem Israel. Besides all this, today is the third day since these things happened. Yes, and certain women of our company, who arrived at the tomb early, astonished us. When they did not find His body, they came saying that they had also seen a vision of angels who said He was alive. And certain of those who were with us went to the tomb and found it just as the women had said; but Him they did not see."

Then He said to them, "O foolish ones, and slow of heart to believe in all that the prophets have spoken! Should not the Christ to have suffered these things and to enter into His glory?"

And beginning at Moses and all the Prophets, He expounded to them in all the Scriptures the things concerning Himself.

The Disciples' Eyes Opened

Then the three drew near to the village where they were going, and He indicated that He would have gone further.

But they constrained Him, saying, "Stay with us, for it is toward evening, and the hour is late."

And He went in to stay with them.

Now, as He sat at the table with them, He took bread, blessed and broke it, and gave it to them. Then their eyes were opened and they knew it was Jesus; and He vanished from their sight.

And they said to one another, "Did not our heart burn within us while He talked with us on the road, and while He opened the Scriptures to us?"

So, they left that same hour and returned to Jerusalem, and found the eleven and those who were with them gathered together, saying, "The Lord is risen, and has appeared to Simon!"

And they told about the things that had happened on the road, and how He was known to them in the breaking of bread.

Jesus Appears to His Disciples

Now as the disciples discussed these things, Jesus Himself stood in the midst of them, and said to them, "Peace to you."

But they were terrified and frightened, and supposed they had seen a spirit.

And Jesus said to them, "Why are you troubled? And why do you have doubts in your hearts? Look, My hands and My feet, that it is I Myself. Handle Me and see, for a spirit does not have flesh and bones as you see I have."

When He had said this, He showed them His hands and His feet.

But while they still did not believe for joy, and marvelled, He said to them, "Have you any food here?"

So, they gave Him a piece of a broiled fish and some honeycomb. And He took it and ate in their presence.

The Scriptures Opened

Then Jesus said to them, "These are the words which I spoke to you while I was still with you, that all things must be fulfilled which were written in the Law of Moses and the Prophets and the Psalms concerning Me."

And He opened their understanding, that they might understand the Scriptures.

Then He said to them, "It is written, and it was necessary for the Christ to suffer and to rise from the dead the third day, and that repentance and remission of sins should be preached in His name to all nations, beginning at Jerusalem. And you are witnesses of these things. I send the Promise of My Father upon you; but stay in the city of Jerusalem until you are filled with power from on high."

Seeing and Believing

Now Thomas, called the Twin, one of the twelve, was not with them when Jesus came. The other disciples said to him, "We have seen the Lord."

So, he said to them, "Unless I see in His hands the print of the nails, and put my finger into the print of the nails, and put my hand into His side, I will not believe."

And after eight days His disciples were again inside, and Thomas with them.

Jesus came, the doors being shut, and stood in the midst, and said, "Peace to you!"

Then He said to Thomas, "Reach your finger here, and look at My hands; and reach your hand here, and put it into My side. Do not be unbelieving, but believing."

And Thomas answered and said to Him, "My Lord and my God!"

Jesus said to him, "Thomas, because you have seen Me, you have believed. Blessed are those who have not seen and yet have believed."

That You May Believe

And truly Jesus did many other signs in the presence of His disciples, which are not written in this book; but these are written that you may believe that Jesus is the Christ, the Son of God, and that believing you may have life in His name.

John 21:1-14

Breakfast by the Sea

After these things Jesus showed Himself again to the disciples at the Sea of Tiberias. These disciples, Simon Peter, Thomas called the Twin, Nathanael of Cana in Galilee, the sons of Zebedee, and two others of His disciples were together. Simon Peter said to them, "I am going fishing."

They said to him, "We are going with you also."

They went out and immediately got into the boat, and that night they caught nothing.

In the morning, Jesus stood on the shore; yet the disciples did not know that it was Jesus.

Jesus said to them, "Children, have you any food?"

They answered Him, "No."

And He said to them, "Cast the net on the right side of the boat, and you will find some."

So, they did as Jesus said, and they were not able to draw in the net because of the multitude of fish.

The disciple whom Jesus loved said to Peter, "It is the Lord!"

Now when Simon Peter heard it was the Lord, he put on his outer garment (for he had removed it), and plunged into the sea. But the other disciples came in the little boat (for they were not far from land, but about two hundred cubits), dragging the net with fish. As soon as they had come to land, they saw a fire of coals there, and fish laid on it, and bread.

Jesus said to them, "Bring some of the fish which you have just caught."

Simon Peter went and joined the others as they dragged the net to land, full of large fish, one hundred and fifty-three; and although there were so many, the net was not broken.

Jesus said to them, "Come and eat breakfast."

None of the disciples dared ask Jesus, "Who are You?", knowing that it was the Lord.

Jesus came and took the bread and gave it to them, and likewise the fish.

This is now the third time Jesus showed Himself to His disciples after He was raised from the dead.

John 21:15-19

Jesus Restores Peter

So, when they had eaten breakfast, Jesus said to Simon Peter, "Simon, son of Jonah, do you love Me more than these?"

He said to Him, "Yes, Lord; You know that I love You."

Jesus said to him, "Feed My lambs."

Jesus said to him again a second time, "Simon, son of Jonah, do you love Me?"

He said to Him, "Yes, Lord; You know that I love You."

Jesus said to him, "Tend My sheep."

Jesus said to him the third time, "Simon, son of Jonah, do you love Me?"

Peter was grieved because Jesus said to him the third time, "Do you love Me?"

And Peter said to Him, "Lord, You know all things; You know that I love You."

Jesus said to him, "Feed My sheep. I say to you, when you were younger, you looked after yourself and walked where you wished; but when you are old, you will stretch out your hands, and another will guide you and carry you where you do not wish."

This Jesus spoke, signifying by what death he would glorify God. And when He had spoken this, He said to him, "Follow Me."

John 21:20-25

The Beloved Disciple and His Book

Then Peter, turning around, saw the disciple whom Jesus loved following, who also had leaned on His breast at the supper, and said, "Lord, who is the one who betrays You?" Peter, seeing him, said to Jesus, "But Lord, what about this man?"

Jesus said to him, "If I will that he remain till I come, what is that to you? You follow Me."

Then this saying went out among the brothers that this disciple would not die. Yet Jesus did not say to him that he would not die, but, "If I will that he remain till I come, what is that to you?"

This is the disciple who testifies of these things, and wrote these things; and we know that his testimony is true. And there are also many other things that Jesus did, which if they were written one by one, I suppose that even the world itself could not contain the books that would be written.

Matthew 28:16-20, Mark 16:14-18

The Great Commission

Later Jesus appeared to the eleven as they sat at the table; and He rebuked their unbelief and hardness of heart, because they did not believe those who had seen Him after He had risen.

Then the eleven disciples went away into Galilee, as far as Bethany, to the mountain which Jesus had appointed for them. When they saw Him, they worshiped Him; but some doubted.

And Jesus came and spoke to them, saying, "All authority has been given to Me in heaven and on earth. Go into all the world and preach the gospel to every creature. He who believes and is baptized will be saved; but he who does not believe will be condemned. And these signs will follow those who believe: In My name, they will cast out demons; they will speak with new tongues; they will take up serpents; and if they drink anything deadly, it will by no means hurt them; they will lay hands on the sick, and they will recover. Go therefore and make disciples of all the nations, baptizing them in the name of the Father and of the Son and of the Holy Spirit, teaching them to observe all things that I have commanded you; and lo, I am with you always, even to the end of the age."

Mark 16:19-20, Luke 24:50-53

The Ascension. Christ Ascends to God's Right Hand

After the Lord had spoken to them, He lifted up His hands and blessed them.

Now, while He blessed them, He was parted from them, received, carried up into heaven, and sat down at the right hand of God.

And the disciples worshiped Him, and returned to Jerusalem with great joy, and were continually in the temple praising and blessing God. And they went out and preached everywhere, the Lord working with them and confirming the word through the accompanying signs. Amen.

Acts 1:1-8

Prologue

The former account I made, O Theophilus, of all that Jesus began both to do and teach, until the day in which He was taken up, after He through the Holy Spirit had given commandments to the apostles whom He had chosen, to whom He also presented Himself alive after His suffering by many infallible proofs, being seen by them during forty days and speaking of the things pertaining to the kingdom of God.

The Holy Spirit Promised

And being assembled together with them, He commanded them not to depart from Jerusalem, but to wait for the Promise of the Father, "which," Jesus said, "you have heard from Me; for John truly baptized with water, but you shall be baptized with the Holy Spirit not many days from now."

For this reason, when they had come together, they asked Him, saying, "Lord, will You at this time restore the kingdom to Israel?"

And Jesus said to them, "It is not for you to know times or seasons which the Father has put in His own authority. But you shall receive power when the Holy Spirit has come upon you; and you shall be witnesses to Me in Jerusalem, and in all Judea and Samaria, and to the end of the earth."

Acts 1:9-26

Jesus Ascends to Heaven

Now when Jesus had spoken these things, while they watched, He was taken up, and a cloud received Him out of their sight. And while they looked steadfastly toward heaven as He went up, two men stood by them in white apparel, who also said, "Men of Galilee, why do you stand gazing up into heaven? This same Jesus, who was taken up from you into heaven, will so come in like manner as you saw Him go into heaven."

The Upper Room Prayer Meeting

Then the disciples returned to Jerusalem from the mount called Olivet, which is near Jerusalem, a Sabbath day's journey.

And when the disciples had entered, they went up into the upper room where they were staying: Peter, James, John, and Andrew; Philip and Thomas; Bartholomew and Matthew; James the son of Alphaeus and Simon the Zealot; and Judas the son of James. These all continued with one accord in prayer and supplication, with the women and Mary the mother of Jesus, and with His brothers.

Matthias Chosen

And in those days Peter stood up in the midst of the disciples (altogether the number of names was about a hundred and twenty), and said, "Men and brothers, this Scripture had to be fulfilled, which the Holy Spirit spoke before by the mouth of David concerning Judas, who became a guide to those who arrested Jesus; for he was numbered with us and obtained a part in this ministry." (Now this man purchased a field with the wages of iniquity; and falling headlong, he burst open in the middle and all his entrails gushed out. And it became known to all those dwelling in Jerusalem; so that field is called in their own language, Akel Dama, that is, Field of Blood.)
"For it is written in the Book of Psalms:

'Let his dwelling place be desolate,
And let no one live in it';

and,

'Let another take his office.'

"For this reason, of these men who have accompanied us all the time that the Lord Jesus went in and out among us, beginning from the baptism of John to that day when Jesus was taken up from us, one of these must become a witness with us of His resurrection."

And they proposed two: Joseph called Barsabas, who was surnamed Justus, and Matthias.

And they prayed and said, "You, O Lord, who know the hearts of all, show which of these two You have chosen to take part in this ministry and apostleship from which Judas by transgression fell, that he might go to his own place."

And they cast their lots, and the lot fell on Matthias. And he was numbered with the eleven apostles.

Acts 2:1-4

Coming of the Holy Spirit

When the Day of Pentecost had fully come, the disciples were all with one accord in one place. And suddenly there came a sound from heaven, as of a rushing mighty wind, and it filled the whole house where they were sitting. Then there appeared to them divided tongues, as of fire, and one sat upon each of them. And they were all filled with the Holy Spirit and began to speak with other tongues, as the Spirit gave them utterance.

Other Books Published by the Author

Cast Your Bread Series

Devotional Talks for the Busy Leader

ISBN: 978-1-4990-3387-8

Easy to read devotionals with all scripture references included.

Bible Studies for the Busy Leader

ISBN: 978-1-5035-0210-9

Easy to follow studies with all relevant scriptures included and referenced.

More Devotional Talks and Bible Studies for the Busy Leader

ISBN: 978-1-5035-0419-6

This edition adds to the many devotions already published.
Other in-depth Bible Studies are added for those exploring the depths of the Bible.

Best Devotions and Bible Studies for the Busy Leader

ISBN: 978-1-5144-9733-3

For those who have searched the mine of God's word, this edition adds further to the previous volumes with all references included for easy reading and study.

Cast Your Bread Series can be purchased on Amazon

The Adventures of Max Series

The Adventures of Max series is based on stories from the Bible and imparts valuable lessons to your children about their connection with God.

All these stories and parables are told through the life of a dog named Max.

Book One: The Defiant Mouse (The Rich Young Ruler)

Book Two: The Curious Chicken (The Lost Sheep)

Book Three: A Dog in Need (The Good Samaritan)

Book Four: An Old Friend Found (The Prodigal Son)

Book Five: The Rescue (The Flood)

Book Six: The Bushfire (Love and Joy Perfected)

Book Seven: A Bad Influence (The Fall of Man)

Book Eight: A Shining Light (I am the Light of the World)

Book Nine: Hidden Secrets (The Parable of the Revealed Light)

Book Ten: A Foiled Plot (The Promised Son)

Book Eleven: Running the Race (The Race of Faith)

Book Twelve: An Unexpected Reward (The Sheep and Goats Revealed)

Book Thirteen: Max Meets a Friend (The Rich Man and Lazarus)

Book Fourteen: Reflections (The Gift of His Peace)

The Adventures of Max series can be purchased online at
www.wittonbooks.com
or from The Adventures of Max Facebook page

Index

Mark's Gospel

Luke's Gospel

John's Gospel

The Acts of the Apostles